My New England

Frank Woolner

Illustrated by Maria Boes

Contents

Stone Wall Country   1
Deep-Freeze Perch   4
The Snow Spirits   8
The Residents   10
Winter Beach   13
Silver Thaw   16
One Bird In Hand   18
The Hunger Moon   21
Springtime Soon   24
The Feather Merchant   26
To All Dogs   29
The Time Clock   32
The Bells Of Springtime   35
First Encounter   37
So Heady A Brew   40
Anglers Are Dreamers   43
Much Magic   45
The Prospectors   48
Melody In The Night   51
Nightcrawler Time   54
Low Key Delight   57
The Night Flyers   61

To Kill A Lake   64
Bug Time   68
Catch Report   71
Elegy For A Ruffed Grouse   74
Sea Change   77
Dr. Doolittle   79
Gone Frogging   82
Bronzeback In The Night   85
The Magic Island   87
Tranquility Regained   90
Summer Interlude   93
Toads Make Warts!   96
Lost Art   99
Salar!   102
The Miracle Workers   105
Turning Point   108
Object: Salmon   111
Of Storm and Stripers   114
The Summer Sniper   118
The Edge Of The Unknown   121
Fall Safari   124
Chinaman's Chance   127
The Rebellious Bees   130
The Eagle Gun   133
'Coon Hunt   136
Line Of Steel   139
Gray Day Relieved   142
Surly Southerner   146
Deerslayer   149
First Ice   152
Rabbit Hunt   154
Conscientious Objector   157
A Christmas Wish   159
Wild Legacy   163

Foreword

My New England is both a place and a state of mind, sometimes hard to fathom, but rarely boring: it is a rugged symphony of rocky pastures and choppy, birch-clad hills where partridges sun and deer flaunt white flags; it is a cold, immortal sea crashing against a coast steeped in tradition. One can always chuckle at the State o' Mainer who visited California. "It's nice," he admitted, "considerin' that it's three-thousand miles from the ocean."

Scholarly countrymen of this old land exhibit the very quintessence of Yankeedom–men, women and children who reflect the virtues and the faults of their sometimes hostile, often poignantly tender environment. Here is the clipped speech and nasal twang, frugality and wry, rawhide humor–a land of "Make do. Eat it up. Wear it out!"

There have been, and are with us now, a fine sprinkling of star-splitters–but New England is casual about her great men, taking them for granted and accepting eccentricity as a right. Thoreau was a dissenter and an erudite radical 125 years before today's crop of long-haired world shakers appeared on the scene. Henry had long hair, too, and in *Walden* he declared: "I have lived some thirty years on this planet, and I have yet to hear the first syllable of valuable or even earnest advice from my seniors."

We have had our moments and our titans, from "First Encounter" to Robert Frost taking that road less traveled by. Grand humans and a leavening of rascals. Cotton Mather in his long black gown, and Samuel Adams building a cradle for liberty; Black Bellamy pirating out of Wellfleet in the *Widah,* and Oliver Wendell Holmes pontificating on the Supreme Court while he wrote poetry of nights. Dan'l Webster and Ralph Waldo Emerson, Calvin Coolidge—and Emily Dickinson, that almost unbelievable wraith who eschewed all worldly things and wrote verses like divine cobwebs spangled with dew.

New England has been, and may still be, a citadel of pure reason in the East. Barring Haight-Asbury sections of Boston and a few other smog-bound, brainwashed centers where the drop-outs clot like swarming bees, we honor individuality, scorn the parrot line and think for ourselves. We deny romanticism, and yet we are great lovers—not of the flesh, but of a bountiful world where humankind and nature intermeshes.

Who gives me leave to write of such a land? Nobody, really. I take that right precisely because I am a New England Yankee, stubbornly satisfied with a natal springboard. My roots are here, twisted into the stone walls and nurtured by a salt sea. I have forgotten my ancient lineage, which goes back to Scotland and England some five generations past. I am as Damn-Yankee as woodbine on the frost-heaved walls of Concord or the statue of a fisherman indomitably facing the dread Atlantic in Gloucester.

Moreover, I was very lucky in a choice of mothers. Mine did something of value early in the game: she provided classics for our reading—and offered no opposition when we pressed ferns and butterflies between their pages. Often, nowadays, rereading a tattered copy of Nathanial Hawthorne's *The House Of The Seven Gables,* or Scott's *The Lady Of The Lake,* or Dickens (for some reason never a favorite) a long-pressed wild geranium or the wing of a yellow swallowtail spills out. In spite of stain, the stuff of genius remains in those pages and I am overcome with a wave of nostalgia for a paradise dimly recalled, a small boy's Nirvana where the fields were always carpeted with buttercups and life was a blessing from hay-scented dawn to flaming sunset. Thanks to a book that will never die because its author was a titan—and a flattened, faded trophy gathered nearly 50 years ago.

In *this* book, which I hope some boy or girl will read with pleasure, and then use to press wildflowers, I touch on seasonal subjects from the viewpoint of an outdoorsman, the almost painfully lovely everyday warp and woof of New England in all seasons. I make no apology for being a gunner and an angler, but I am a hunter without malice and maybe a fisher who seeks much more than any limit catch of trout.

It should be noted that there are, among sportsmen, a minority of dolts who assume that killing is the name of the game. Usually they learn better, as the years march on and the magic of creation touches them. Actually, the hunter and the angler are Nature's best friends: they harvest a small crop—and fight like cornered tigers for good management of land, water, the beasts thereon and the fishes in stream or sea. They put their money where their mouth is.

Granted, a New England sportsman boasts about great days in the uplands, about doubles on grouse and center shots at whitetail deer. He is, in his own mind, a hairy-chested outdoorsman—deadly with a gun and always capable of limiting-out on the jeweled brook trout that were here before the Vikings made landfall.

Yet, at one and the same time, he is the gentlest of earth's lovers. If he takes a towering woodcock in October, he will be first to protest an industrial development that threatens a spring singing ground. He is wise in birds and protects them. He knows where the wildflowers bloom and makes annual pilgrimages to observe the first marsh marigolds, yellow violets and ladyslippers. In due time he becomes a specialist, scorning the easy kill and setting his own sparse bag limits—often well below those decreed by law.

I see a definite evolution. As boys, those of us who are wedded to this lovely, rock-studded land are worshippers at the shrine of rod and gun. Our avowed desire is to kill more game and catch more fish than anyone down the road, and often we succeed. That is part of the exuberance of youth.

Sliding into maturity, there is the happy phenomenon of specialization and conservation of all natural resources. Suddenly no trout is worthy unless it is taken on a fly and released to fight again. One or two great game birds assume paramount importance, and a true zealot will case his guns if he feels that a quarry has been over-harvested. One finds a vital need to check the nests of brown thrashers and orioles, to track winter animals for no other purpose than curiosity and secret joy in reading a story written in new snow.

He'd never admit it, but such a man (women readily admit such things) is in love with the country and the things that make it desirable in all seasons. There is something indescribably delicious about clean swamp mud and the pungent perfume of a working farm, things soul-satisfying in birdsong and frogs chunking and bees sampling a field of clover. There is cold magic in an ice storm and the deep, soft drift of snow stitched with elfin tracks of field mice.

Know this, and know it very certainly: a man or a woman born in New England will never be completely happy anywhere else on earth. In his dreams, if not in reality, this is "the place to return to, to be buried in."

So it is my land and I have written about it for my own joy–and hopefully for the laconic, nodded approval of contemporaries. These slices of life, for the most part, were originally printed in the "Feature Parade" of the Worcester, Massachusetts *Sunday Telegram,* and I thank the editors of that newspaper for permission to present them here.

The series was launched when the late Frederick Rushton, a grand editor, asked me to do something I had never remotely contemplated. "Give me a timely column of outdoor impressions, first person," he said. "Make it accurate, keyed to the season, the flavor of the countryside with no holds barred."

First person is tough for a New England Yankee. We are tight-lipped people, not much given to displaying our emotions and always embarrassed when discovered in the act of love. We have a strangely Puritan aversion to admitting any tenderness or delight. We are charlatans of the first order.

But not charlatans where truth is concerned. Everything noted here actually occurred. While I have consulted the books to insure the accuracy of scientific names and spelling–I am an abominable speller–I have also spent a happy lifetime associating with New England's wildlife and fish and woodlands and flowers.

I admit to being in love with New England: it is one of the most densely populated areas of America, and yet there remain vast reaches of aboriginal woodlands, crystalline waters, meadows and swamps within its borders. We have the shouldering sea, clean, cold and often menacing. Grouse still drum in the warm dawns of May, and the squaretail trout rises in opal-tinted sunset light. There are whitetail deer feeding among the half-wild cows in June, and lordly bucks pawing the hardwood ridges in November. Magnificent game fishes course our salt coast, and the stars are still close and burning when you can escape the cities.

My New England goes a long way back, spiced with personal recollection and colored by dreams in the long night watches after action. I am delightfully hag-ridden by nostalgia–fields of dandelions and Queen Anne's lace, ripe cherries on the Fourth of July and an Atlantic salmon served with new green peas for dinner. There is nothing better than the sounds and sights and smells of a backwoods hunting camp, regardless of kill. I like apple blossoms foaming in the spring and red maples flaming in the fall.

All of these things, and so many more. White birches, bowed by ice storms, and little, tucked-away valley farms where it is still possible to buy warm milk topped with yellow cream. I am forever awed by stone walls marching across mountains and by cellar holes that mark homesteads returned to the jungle before my grandfathers were born. I dote on a whippoorwill in springtime and a chickadee that shares a hunter's lunch in November. All of it is right, and all of it is nice.

So I tell it as I see it, week by week throughout the tumultuous year. Doesn't everyone, regardless of domicile, have a little of New England in his soul?

F. W.
1972

Acknowledgments

I am indebted to some very good friends in the newspaper business and in the vineyards of outdoor writing. The late Frederick L. Rushton, feature editor of the Worcester *Sunday Telegram,* Worcester, Massachusetts initially conceived and commissioned a series of articles in first person, each to do with a sportsman's love affair with the out-of-doors. Later, that fine newspaper's publisher was kind enough to bless the inclusion of these vignettes in a new book.

My brothers, Jack Woolner and Dick Woolner, have been enthusiastic co-workers in joyous research.

Horace G. "Tap" Tapply, of New Hampshire and *Field & Stream* magazine, offered much encouragement. Since Tap was one of my first mentors in the craft of outdoor writing, and especially because he is a master story-teller, his commendation was gratifying.

I am beholden to wonderful companions in the field, many of whom are mentioned in this book. They are hunters, fishermen, farmers, naturalists and gentle bird watchers. Their philosophy is not always mine, but we agree on basics.

New England is our chosen land: we all desire to maintain an ecology, an environment and a tradition we hold second to none.

Finally, I am indebted to Maria Boes for illustrating this little volume. She has added a lacy, somehow old-world patina–and that is entirely right because, even after 350-odd years of residence, every New England Yankee remains a wide-eyed newcomer in a new world.

Frank Woolner
August 1972

Stone Wall Country

Intrigued by new snow on a mild winter morning, I followed a deer that jumped in a slashing and evaded pursuit by ambling over a convenient mountain. The fact that I dogged this whitetail, alternately peering at its tracks and then scanning the hardwoods ahead, is of no account.

It was wild country. Tall oaks and paper birches reached for the sky. Conifers towered and the second growth was too thick for comfort. After a couple of hours, noting that the deer was still moving rapidly, I quit. Then, far back in the woods, I found a great elm growing in an ancient cellar hole.

The tree was mature, massive at the butt, so it had been there—as my grandfather used to say—"a right smart time." Maybe three times as long as I've been alive.

New England boasts thousands of cellar holes in the wilderness. Some of them date back to the American Revolution, and some to an indefinite period before or after the Gold Rush of '49. Each is a memorial to a civilization that burgeoned and died before the West was settled.

Once, long ago, this northern jungle was cleared and planted to corn, wheat and such almost forgotten apples as the russet and baldwin. Then the runty cattle of our pioneers were confined by multitudinous skeins of stone walls.

1

They are everywhere in our Yankee woods, gray and solid, like something evolved by nature. Stone walls crisscrossing wooded hills. Stone walls meandering through a wilderness. Always the walls, straight and symmetrical, mute testimony to the muscle-busting labor of forgotton landsmen. Were they walling themselves in? Or others out?

Robert Frost noted that "good fences make good neighbors," and maybe that was it. Still, timber was ample and rails would have confined stock as well as stone. Was something of religious fervor involved? Our forefathers counted hard labor most virtuous. Lord, what labor!

The land was cleared, then, and today's game trail up a mountainside was a rutted cartroad. They prised the great boulders out of cornfield and pasture, levered them on to stone boats—a sort of dry land toboggan. Oxen and horses strained to drag heavy loads to the wall-sites, where trenches had been ploughed to receive the foundation stones.

How many tortuous man-hours went into this chore, and how much skill? Consider those massive foundations, topped by carefully fitted keystones, with rubble in the center. How many heart attacks and hernias are built into the vast loops and chains of stone that characterize the countryside of New England?

They are long gone, those sinewy, bearded farmers—many of them sleeping in clasped-hand repose under the towering elms that were seedlings when they lived and tilled the land. Now graceful birches arch overhead and woodbine complements the weathered piles. Deer pause to munch wild raspberry shoots, and squirrels count the walls their sylvan highways.

Two thousand years hence, if our suicidal civilization has in the interim managed to extinguish itself in a blaze of nuclear fission, the new breed may find these skeins of granite and puzzle over their uses, just as modern man marvels at the strange enigma of Stonehenge.

At any rate, the walls are as much a part of New England as white birches and colonial architecture, hourglass elms and Concord Bridge. They are durable monuments to men who conquered a wilderness, and a reminder that the wilderness returns.

I failed to see my deer on this high, clear morning, but I followed an immaculate stone wall down a mountainside—and the shades of the pioneers went with me. In spite of our teeming cities and suburban sprawl, we live in an old land.

Deep-Freeze Perch

Springtime may be an impossible dream when temperatures plummet and the flinty cold of late January nightly adds layers of ice over ponds already sheathed in a foot of glass-hard armor. Yet the signs are there.

Reluctantly, I had agreed to go ice fishing with a brother who works for the Massachusetts Department of Natural Resources, and who therefore waxes enthusiastic about angling in all seasons. In addition to which—he needed some motion pictures of people hauling fish through a hole in the ice.

Now logically I hold it ridiculous to submit to arctic winds, stone-cracking temperatures and heavy labor for the dubious pleasure of catching a few yellow perch. Fortunately, ice fishing is one of a very few endeavors which prove better in the doing than in anticipation.

Swathed in goosedown parkas and heavy boots, equipped with razor-edged chisels and jigging sticks, we bent into the stinging wind which whistled across a little Yankee pond. At least, I thought gloomily, the sky was blue and a frosty sun was swinging low over pine-clad horizons. There might have been sleet or a blizzard.

Spudding a hole through 12 inches of ice is guaranteed to promote a measure of circulation, so the cold became almost bearable after a half-hour of alternate chopping and walking. Presently we reached a shallow bar where the bottom was clearly outlined under six feet of water. Pale green weeds undulated over white sand and–quite suddenly–fish-shaped shadows moved in this natural aquarium.

Jack crowed with delight as his jigging stick bent double and he hauled a ten inch perch into the sunlight. By the time he'd iced a second, I'd forgotten the cold and the wind. There was nothing in that pale blue world but the spur of competition.

Completely dedicated to the task at hand, I watched my jigging spoon zigzag down, felt it touch bottom and then break free as I took a turn on the reel spool. Presently there was a jolt–missed–and another, followed by writhing weight.

A yellow perch is a democratic fish, ready to oblige at any season. I think the species is best in midwinter, at a time when brilliant color and flashing action too often is memory.

So I was excited! My perch came spiraling up, fighting all the way; it was hauled out of the spud hole in a little geyser of flying water and ice chips, and it flopped heroically–a magnificent, plump midget marked with living color.

Yellow perch are advanced members of their genus, well shaped and pugnacious in appearance. Perhaps the ground color is yellow, but I say gold, with black bars. Anal and pectoral fins are bright red.

Fortunately for winter anglers, perch travel in schools: when you find one, others are likely to be present in surprising numbers. An angler can reef out five or six in succession before the school moves on, and then it is only necessary to spud holes to right or left in order to find the traveling gamesters.

Fevered with action, we left our captives where they had fallen on the ice, and we fanned out to port and starboard. Again, Jack found them and I moved in to share the bonanza. Curiously, the weather seemed to have moderated: I found myself tucking gloves in a handy pocket and unzipping the goosedown parka.

Presently we had enough for an old fashioned fish fry—and no inland species is better than the white-fleshed perch after a session on a buttered grill. On hands and knees we watched as the tiny metal spoons plummeted down.

Yellow perch can be exasperating, or they may bite like prisoners of war exposed to sirloin steaks. These approached our lures, surveyed them, backed off–and then seemed to move within a half-inch of the dancing spoons.

There was no mad charge, simply an outward telescoping of jaws

and (evidently) a suction which propelled the light artificial into the mouth of the fish. If the hook was not set immediately the perch would discharge the lure—and that particular perch, we thought, would not come back.

Finally, Jack and I retraced our steps, harvesting the catch. By now our coats were open and the temperature seemed almost balmy. Nobody is healthier than a spudder and, maybe, nobody is happier.

Exertion had warmed our blood, but the cold was evident. Each perch was immobile, victim of the January deep-freeze, and arrested in an attitude of life with fins flared, gills distended and body arched.

Some were long and slim, while others—the more colorful—seemed impossibly deep bodied and plump. These latter specimens were females, distended with roe. That caviar of New England and the entire north country would be a gourmet's delight on tomorrow's dinner table.

But it reminded us that springtime was more than a dream. These perch were already seeking the shallows, sensing the wheeling seasons, somehow aware that another six weeks would see open water and a time to deposit dainty, gelatinous eggs on water weeds and submarine brush.

Therefore it was an adventure for us—and a lesson in the ecology of perch. We went out cold and came back perspiring. We'd had a great day—with one exception. Jack forgot to take any pictures.

I suppose we'll have to go back.

The Snow Spirits

That morning I had hoped to seek cottontail rabbits with a handgun, but the sky was dark at dawn, streaked by an ominous stain of red in the East. By 8 a.m. the first snowflakes were sifting down. Evidently the weather forecasters were right for a change: a January blizzard was beginning.

Any sane man remains at home in such weather, and I was normal enough to resist the urge to travel–but good intentions suffer when some untoward incident triggers the imagination. It was a snowy owl that proved my undoing.

Standing at a picture window, watching the almost horizontal slant of this wind-driven storm, I saw the owl soar over a nearby pasture. He–or perhaps she, for I haven't the foggiest notion of vital distinctions in the plumage of this northern visitor–came to rest on a fence post.

So, of course, it was necessary to don shoe-pacs and a parka–to plunge out into the whistling fury of the blizzard to renew acquaintances.

As usual, the Arctic owl seemed curiously disdainful of mankind. I'd slogged to within 30 yards before he lifted into the wind and went soaring away, skimming a few feet over the ground and following its contours.

That was quite enough time to absorb the wide glare of yellow eyes and the fine barring of brown over pure white plumage. He was a big bird, probably fluffed up against the chill, but certainly equal to our native barred owl in size.

At the moment I should have returned to the warmth of a suburban office, but the drifting dunes on a winter pasture seemed to beckon. Stricken spikes of goldenrod and hardhack resisted the covering. Shrubs and trees cowered before a blast of fine snow particles. For a time no living thing moved, and there were no tracks of deer mice or cottontail rabbits. Nature observes a moritorium in a blizzard.

Strike that last sentence and make it read: "resident" wildlife retreats during a great snowfall. The owl was vibrantly alive in our elemental fury, and now I witnessed a veritable flurry of small birds.

Somewhat larger than English sparrows, they were all buff and brown and white. A ragged gaggle of them arose and seemed to be blown by the demonic wind. The thin tinkle of their voices drifted back. Snow buntings! Snowbirds—or, as some like to call them, "snowflakes."

Therefore I trudged another mile, snow trickling into my boots, the zero blast pinching my ears, strangely elated in a howling blizzard. Something had gone entirely right!

The owl and the snow buntings had come down out of arctic fastnesses, each for a similar reason, yet totally unlike in nature. My owl would capture and eat a "snowflake" wherever possible, and he would be quite ruthless in the destruction of native pheasants and cottontail rabbits. He was a day flier, an ominous whiteness in a swirl of white, and this frigid Yankee land of mine, was, for him, a southern vacation area.

The snow buntings are seed eaters, not predators, but—again—our northern New England uplands and pastures must seem a promised land when contrasted with the icy deep-freeze of North America's true Arctic.

Once, many years ago when I was a barbaric youth and a student of taxidermy, I killed snow buntings and mounted them as trophies. In those days every hunter counted the slaughter of an Arctic owl a high spot in his career. Times surely change.

This was a day made memorable simply because I had seen these visitors from the far North. We had arranged a confrontation, thanks to the storm, and none of us had suffered any ill. For once a blizzard had its good points.

The Residents

Kipling said: "Only mad dogs and Englishmen go out in the mid-day sun."

Twist that declaration to our northern wintertime and you may come up with an observation that only rabbit hunters and naturalists challenge a New England blizzard.

I had a day of no particular work, and quite naturally *The Law of General Cussedness* insured heavy snowfall. It was a time to read by a blazing fire, for the roads were still unplowed. I chose to don winter woolens and shoe-pacs, to strike out into our suburban wilderness and read the tracks of the wild creatures.

By 10 a.m. the storm had degenerated into fitful gusts of snow. Sunlight was making a valiant effort to pierce low cloud, and the trees were rigid, extending their wiry branches into a cold, gray sky. Our days might be lengthening, but the north country seemed gripped in a deep-freeze. Could any wildlife survive?

In mid-January the woods seem sterile, clothed in white and apparently untenanted. At first glance one might assume that life has vanished, but I assure you that the initial impression is entirely erroneous. Wild creatures flourish in cold and snow. Those species which have acclimated themselves to our sometimes inhospitable northland go about their business with an insouciance bordering upon gaiety.

Human beings fret in snowtime, but the creatures of the wilderness accept elemental fury as part of life's pattern. While a blizzard beats across our Yankee landscape, life pauses. Deer bed down in thick conifers. Grouse roost in hollowed-out chambers under the accumulated drifts.

No bird or mammal, other than storm-loving juncoes and snow buntings, challenge the elements. Philosophically, the citizens of our woodlands and fields passively wait for better days.

But let the storm abate and there is no drowsy interlude of snowbound inaction. I think that the wild creatures are finely attuned to barometric pressures, and that is why the period immediately after elemental fury finds our near-wilderness fully awake and active. There is no better time to conduct a census of winter birds and beasts than those hours following a blizzard.

Initially, the chickadees were ecstatic as they searched for weed seeds and the eggs of long-gone summer insects cached in the bark of winter's tree trunks. These black-capped acrobats may well appear at suburban bird feeders, but they are perfectly capable of living in the wild.

The great thing about an immediate post-storm survey is the knowledge that any track will be brand new. Observation of an animal's signature in fresh snow is the next best thing to seeing the creature, for tracks tell a complete story.

Almost immediately I found the spoor of a cottontail rabbit, the clay still fresh where he had emerged from a woodchuck's burrow and shook brown earth from his fluffy coat. I didn't see him in person, but there were the marks of chisel teeth where he had stripped the bark from a snow-burdened branch of wild apple.

Fortunately, that was a warning: I'd almost forgotton about the cottontail's hunger moon and now remembered a flowering olive shrub that had best be circled with wire mesh to defeat the sharp teeth of starving rodents.

In addition, I made a mental note to offer nightly appeasement in the shape of apples. Feed cottontails and you will find them unlikely to destroy valuable shrubs.

Before the sun had burst through our overcast, the whole woodland was stitched with tracks. Gray squirrels were crisscrossing the oak woods, burrowing for acorns. Field mice had skittered from one clump of grass to another. There was the direct, fastidious spoor of a red fox—and a point where a ruffed grouse had defeated this reiver of the northland by bursting out of a juniper clump.

Best of all, two deer had been pawing ancient, worm-riddled apples out of the leaf mold of an orchard long reverted to wilderness. They couldn't have been more than minutes ahead of me, but I hardly expected to see them—so I backtracked.

These whitetails, probably a doe and her yearling fawn, had bedded on a little knoll with a scrub pine for overhead canopy. Obviously they'd been there through the entire storm, for the beds were oval depressions with dry leaves underneath. I could almost see them there, as they were an hour previously—legs doubled under woods-gray bodies, snowflakes on their black noses and curling eyelashes, passively outwaiting the blizzard. Why had they sought apples long gone to rot and hardly edible? Tracks pose problems.

In the end of it, comfortably weary, I slogged back through the drifts to meet with a neighbor who passed the time of day while he leaned on a shovel.

"Must be pretty hard on wild birds and animals," he suggested.

I agreed, because that seemed the thing to do. Good citizens pity the wild creatures in wintertime and fail to realize that our northern birds and mammals were here before we came to make their lives more difficult.

They're the true residents, and we're the shivering immigrants.

Winter Beach

It has been said, and perhaps I am guilty of it too, that frontiers are now confined to outer space and the deep sea bed. In a way, this is true—but any human being who nurses the spark of adventure may visit a lost land.

Always, in mid-winter, I cherish a trip to the outer beaches of Cape Cod. In January, this summer playground of bikini-clad bathers and boatmen and anglers is almost as remote as the pitted surface of the moon. No man's footprints mar the packed sand, and no beach buggy tracks wind through the shifting dunes.

Now humankind has retreated—back into the teeming cities and the sleepy Cape towns. If an ice-encrusted dragger tramps out and back, butting through arctic spray, she can only add to a pale seascape. Almost nobody prospects the long beaches in January.

I had planned to hunt scoters and eiders, the marine waterfowl that are commonly called "sea coots." Skeins of them had been working up and down the coast, trading over yeasty waters. Unfortunately for me, as a gunner, this happened to be a bluebird day. There was no ground swell to speak of and the wind was as gentle as a kiss.

But, after all it was January and the dune grass hoarded patches of snow. I racked my shotgun and turned the Jeep's blunt snout south of Provincetown, into the fastnesses of Cape Cod's National Seashore.

Far over the dunes a gout of industrial smoke spiraled into a still sky. Overhead, a high flying jet left contrails. There were several beach shacks, deserted in the bitter days of mid-winter–and then nothing but a sweep of shore, apparently aboriginal.

We dote on the internal combustion engine, but where there are no tracks and no evidences of mankind, a driver tenses for the slightest sound of mechanical failure. I kept to the high dunes, ignoring easier going on hard-packed flats–because I knew that the sea would come surging back on its appointed rounds. Behind me, the Jeep's track was etched like a steel engraving. No one had blazed this trail.

On our raving North Atlantic coast, the open ocean runs amok in wintertime. I found a spot where gouging nor'easters had cut the beach into scalloped formations, digging into the anchoring grass where it marched down from bayberry covered uplands. July's beach buggies would have to detour here. Or would they?

One storm ravages, and another builds. The hugh piece bitten out of a headland might well be replaced by the shifting sands of another natural cataclysm. January's dune formations provide no hint of a new summer's topography.

Somewhere between Race Point and Highland Light, encouraged by the Jeep's steady purr, I clawed up to a high dune and cut the ignition. Below me, the ocean was as serene and blue as ever it was when anglers launched their small boats to hunt for stripers in July.

The sound was unchanged. Ground swells rose slowly, crested, and rushed in upon the unyielding shore. There was the same hiss and rapidly building climactic crash as the wave exploded in bright foam and went racing up the shingle. There was that well remembered receding broken-glass tinkle of rocks and sea shells and sand as the undertow drew its breath.

Below me the bones of a dragger–crushed here in a winter storm of years before–jutted out of hard-packed sand. To my certain knowledge that boat's skeleton has been buried and exhumed time after time. It is a landmark, seen or unseen, a monument to man's impotence before the raging ocean.

Far offshore, secure in calm weather, strings of scoters and eiders flowed across the horizon. Once a pair of black ducks orbited high overhead, craning their astute heads to examine my Jeep. With the exception of waterfowl, it seemed a biological desert, but I dismounted to prospect.

Here were the concentric wind-tracks of dune grass tips circling each clump, sharply etched in sand. Here, also, were the elfin footprints of mice stitching the distances between hummocks and bayberry islands.

A deer had come down through a low jungle of rose pips and beach plums, probably seeking the salt of the sea. And, as authoritative as any signature, there was the mark of a fox overlaying a cottontail rabbit's powder-puff spoor. Even in mid-winter the sea-rim is alive, pulsing with life.

Presently I cranked up and followed an old track through the beaten-down grass. There was a gap in the high dunes; beyond it, herring gulls were riding the wind, probably circling a town dump. Their white underwings glistened in hard sunlight, but they weren't looking for baitfish under stripers now. All of that, in January, was long ago and far away—as remote as the anglers of August.

In fact, aside from a broken lobster trap trailing a frayed length of hemp, windrows of planks and hewn timbers cast up on a strangely virgin beach, there was nothing to speak of mankind and little of other living creatures.

Not, that is, until the Jeep swivelled around a little point, throwing sand from all four clutching wheels. Dead ahead, stark and silver-gray, a gnarled hunk of driftwood was anchored in the dunes. On its apex a great white Arctic owl surveyed the wintry world with cold yellow eyes.

He was a wraith in a wasteland, and I braked hard while I reached for binoculars. This creature had migrated out of the far North, famished when native forage had failed. Now he was coursing our Cape, preying on waterfowl and small mammals, scavenging dead fish and devouring whatever the flowing tides might deliver.

Of course I let him go in peace, for he had come far and he had provided a wonderful finale for a probe into a lost frontier.

Silver Thaw

As usual, it started with a mid-winter thaw and a cold, misty rain which coincided with steadily dropping temperatures. The liquid film froze upon contact, hence every branch and twig built its own armor of clear ice.

Long before dawn a cold front had pushed that storm out over the Atlantic. By sun-up our north country was immersed in an elemental deep-freeze. It was magnificent. No outdoorsman can afford to sleep on the first morning of an ice storm.

The existing snow cover offered no problem: it was light and glazed with ice. Before I'd donned heavy woolens and rubber-bottomed shoe-pacs for a journey of reconnaissance, my brother, Dick, discovered a ruffed grouse under an apple tree at the end of our lawn.

The grouse was all fluffed up, insulated against the cold. As big as a football, it strutted beneath the tree, picked at infinitesimal weed seeds and finally meandered into a grotesque jungle of ice-coated brush.

Until the wind rises, such a jungle is a mixture of incomparable beauty and Alice-in-Wonderland vistas. Diamonds may be a girl's best friends, but no courtesan ever witnessed jewelry to match that strung on every twig during the first hours of a true silver thaw.

A deep-freeze is silent, so you must go shortly after dawn on a first day to appreciate a countryside completely imprisoned and fixed at a moment of struggle. It's a brittle world's end–truly magnificent–and bearable only because you know it can't last.

The color of such a day defies description. Sunlight sets the entire universe ablaze. Each stand of white birches, bowed like a field of wheat under a tornadic wind, reflects a multitude of flaming hues from bejeweled topgallants. White light and shadow, together with refraction, generate flashes of ruby and emerald, pure translucent silver and subtle lavender. No gem of great price ever burns so bright or exists for so short a time.

Entranced, I battered through a lacy wilderness of fine spun glass. Shards of ice chattered as they fell. There were no birds, no bouncing cottontails, no sign of the multitudinous life I knew existed in this wood.

They were there, of course–everything from the chickadee roosting in a conifer to the deer bedded in a thicket. They could afford to wait for Nature to loosen her iron grip. Wild creatures are programmed to such periods of chill and famine. The northern birds and mammals have known ice storms for a million years. Only mankind frets.

By 10 a.m. the breeze had freshened. Now our woodlands were a clattering bedlam of sound, of tortured tree trunks and branches recovering their positions after the ice had cracked, shattered and gone plummeting to earth.

By this time the grouse would be feasting, carefully gleaning the fat, male buds of aspen and ignoring the less nutritional female buds. Chickadees would be sure to be picking miniscule grubs from unburdened branches, and deer would be ghosting through the thickets, nibbling shoots of red maple and wild raspberry. The storm was, after all, just one of those things. It was part and parcel of northern wintertime, an event to suffer, to wait out, to enjoy–rarely a tragedy.

Unless, of course, the human intellect counts thousands of dead limbs brought to earth, plus the pruning of poorly grown live limbs a sorrow. Unless, as a human, you honestly dislike the classic, ice-induced curve of white birches.

Come on, now! Any fool knows that a curve is prettier than a straight line.

One Bird in Hand

I don't know whether a bird in hand is worth two in the bush, but a chickadee that perches on my fingertips is much more interesting than a whole squadron of small flyers in the high birches.

That's one reason why a feeder is situated in our suburban back yard. The thing doesn't help winter birds–in fact it probably conditions them to a welfare state, concentrates them in time and space for the benefit of predators, and is otherwise unnecessary.

So I confess to embracing that old nonsense about "helping our feathered friends." Actually, I help myself. Quite simply stated, it is pleasant to observe the different winter visitors and, sometimes, to become closely acquainted.

My birds serve several purposes: they offer a ready-made excuse to leave the typewriter and peer through binoculars. It is well worth deserting gainful labor to identify a laggard towhee, a grumpy evening grosbeak or a purple finch–the latter appearing exactly like a sparrow drenched in port wine. Each new arrival is carefully noted. This is a status thing among us birders. How many species do *you* have?

Best of all, there's something almost painfully delightful in convincing a chickadee that it is quite all right to land on your outstretched fingertips. It is a stellar accomplishment, like scoring a double on grouse or tumbling the duck that your best friend has missed. I suppose I've just lost my bird-watching friends again!

Wayne Hanley of the Massachusetts Audubon Society says there is increasing evidence that some birds return to specific feeders each year, and I think he is right. Wayne knows a lot about birds, and I count him an excellent fellow because he once confided that he was a hunter in his youth. I hope this expose doesn't cost Hanley his job.

At any rate, early winter always finds at least one or two chickadees that come quickly to an outstretched hand full of sunflower seeds. Others flutter in the near vicinity, unable to make up their minds. I think the bold mites remember other years–those of them that have survived hawks, owls and plagues of pesticide.

Even lacking old campaigners, anyone can teach a chickadee to eat out of his hand. All it takes is patience and the ability to keep still. This may sound elementary, but for some reason the human animal places immobility on a par with levitation.

Just grab a handful of sunflower seeds and repair to a place where chickadees are plentiful–such as the vicinity of a winter feeder. Next, extend arm and hand, palm up. *Don't move.*

If the birds are spooky–and maybe they've been harassed by small boys with BB guns, cuddly domestic kitty-cats and an assortment of courageous lap dogs–there'll be a deal of close inspection and jittery flight. *Don't move.*

If necessary, and usually it is, brace your arm against a handy tree trunk or against the feeder itself. Pretty soon a chickadee will touch down on your outstretched fingertips and you'll feel the grip of his tiny, wiry claws. *Don't move.*

After that, you've got it made. If one chickadee finds that a man (or a woman) can be trusted, others will follow. Those black, beady little eyes miss nothing. Presently the neighbors will think that you have some strange power over birds. Indeed, if you persevere, in no time at all you'll have a cab-rank of birds coming to your outstretched palm at every appearance.

Wayne Hanley says nothing about chickadees recognizing specific people, but I have one with a sharply cocked, inquisitive head. He looks just like the weary traveler who landed on my shoulder some ten miles south of Martha's Vineyard in late October. That time, out on the roaring ocean, I had no sunflower seeds–so the bird departed, leaving a small memento on our fishing boat's deck.

Rightly, too, for a chickadee deserves some reward when he's brave enough to make friends with a human being.

The Hunger Moon

Two short months hence the woodlands of our north country will be teeming with life, but now the hardwood aisles are still and the big swamps seem barren under their armor of snow and ice. February is the Hunger Moon of the Yankee wilderness, the sterile ebb tide of the seasons.

Now all of the wild creatures are weary of winter rations, lean of flank and struggling to sustain life itself until the first green shoots of springtime signal a return to abundance. The struggle is progressive.

In December, for example, there were five cottontails at my back door. They came each evening, just as the last yellow-green rays of sunset touched the bare maples. They came because I spread a nightly feast of apples—and still do. Well-fed rabbits rarely eat ornamental shrubs.

By mid-January there were four, and then—last week—only three. Obviously, the ruthless attrition of this bitter period is taking its annual toll.

Few birds or mammals escape the casualty lists of wintertime. Ringnecked pheasants diminish in numbers as the season wanes. Ruffed grouse, gray squirrels and varying hares become less plentiful as the weakest among them succumb to cold weather and predation. There is a definite winter-kill, a thinning-out which cannot be controlled by mankind.

Once my home coverts in central Massachusetts sustained a flourishing population of quail. These handsome little game birds survived gunning pressures and the decimation of wintertime until several successive years of abnormally heavy snowfall and arctic weather practically exterminated them.

Whitetail deer are perennial victims of the ebb tide season. If the snow is very deep and the deer are yarded, fawns of the year will die of starvation–because they are not tall enough to reach available browse.

Snow, particularly crusted snow, dictates a new peril. Roving dog packs are now able to drive the weakened deer to exhaustion and to pull them down in a welter of blood and guts. It is a shocking thing to see, and yet it is a hallmark of the season. A deer is a run-and-stop animal, while dogs never halt. The end is inevitable.

Dogs, deep snow and crust combine to insure this tragedy, but mortality would still be light were it not for iron rations. Deer are close to starvation this month: they no longer possess the vibrant stamina of summer and fall, so they become easier victims for the killers.

If an outdoorsman learns anything by tramping the woods, it is that Nature gives and takes with equal profligacy. There is no easy existence for wild creatures–yet this may be the very source of their strength and resilience. February thins the ranks, but those left to maintain the race are an elite. Survival of the fittest is no idle phrase in winter woodlands.

Sometimes, though, it seems a bitterly close contest, frustrating to a human being because of his helplessness. One can feed a few hungry birds and animals–at the cost of concentrating them in time and space–thus obliging equally hungry predators. No man can conquer the attrition of the winter wilderness, and perhaps it would be unwise to do so even if this were possible. Nature has her own checks and balances.

February, since the dawn of time in our north country, has been a dark month for wild creatures. Fortunately, the Indian's Hunger Moon also offers a faint promise of better things to come.

Although ice booms across our lakes and snow still lies deep in the black growth, horned owls are beginning to shout in the night. The great owls are mating and building their nests. Score one for spring and for the miraculous renewal of wildlife which is always preceded by grim struggle in February.

Springtime Soon

Always I expect too much of March. There is no earthly reason why the flip of a calendar page should dissipate cold winds and driving snow. In our north country this third month is far from springlike, but I'll never learn.

So, stubborn as any rock-ribbed Yankee, I slogged out into a suburban wilderness. The big swamps were frozen solid and frost held the earth in a vice-like grip.

There were deer tracks in a back orchard, with the prints of dogs superimposed. Late winter is a time of travail for the whitetail. Does are now heavy with fawn, yet emaciated after a long Hunger Moon. The snow-cover supports pursuing dogs, while deer labor and break through—a perennial tragedy.

This day I went armed, just to feel the heft of a gun tugging at my belt. It was a .357 magnum revolver, patterned after Colt's famous Peacemaker. The thing can deliver a well-aimed slug on target at 200 yards, but I am not marksman enough to do this. Moreover, I planned to kill nothing: if the gun were fired, it would probably be a matter of target practice on some remote hillside.

There is no dramatic change as February slides into March. When the north wind soughs through somber pines and bare maples, you might as well be back in January. It's cold. One hardly looks for any touch of spring, so each sign of renewal is doubly precious.

First, in the clean, harsh light of early afternoon I saw crows circling and performing aerobatics above a grove of white pines. Crows become slightly addled in the spring, when romance turns their usually astute heads.

Thereafter, and perhaps one sees what he wants to see, I rested on an old stone wall that skirts a ridge and overlooks a great swamp. The cold gray and white shades were there, but a guttering sun seemed to awaken some faint flush of red in the branches and buds of bare maples. Color comes first, and then burgeoning growth. A hint, no matter how slight, is important in March.

Convinced, I trudged down out of the scrub oaks to cross a ploughed field where the late winter sun had exposed waves of frost-crystalled mud above a dying snow cover. A muskrat had traveled this way, his scrabbling tracks cleanly etched. Knowing muskrat nature, I could almost see this angry, furred creature rebelling against winter—deserting the waterways to seek terrestrial foodstuffs. Surprise a muskrat in the fields, in March, and he'll likely charge you—chattering furiously!

It was cold as the sun descended, a winter dusk that denied any hope of springtime. I turned homeward, following a power line where walking was easiest. Below me, a point of woodland suddenly disgorged a running deer followed by three dogs–a beagle, a dubious collie and a nondescript mongrel. Silently, almost mechanically, they loped after the whitetail. This was a chase that could only end in tragedy unless the killers were turned aside. For the first time that day I found a need for my big handgun.

I didn't try to kill. The first shot boomed like an artillery piece in the still countryside. I saw the heavy slug strike well ahead of the leading beagle. Another round sent a plume of snow towering–and the dogs halted. After that it was easy to shout them into retreat. Maybe I'd saved a deer.

Yet, Lord, it was cold–and there was no sign of spring, save a recollection of crows tumbling, and a muskrat's tracks, and a hint of color in the swamp maples. I might as well have been cruising a mid-winter woodland.

But I knew better, and so did the dogs and so did the deer. March means springtime soon, in spite of the elements and in spite of general appearances.

The Feather Merchant

A pox on all who wait for opening day to go fishing! I think March is a prime time for anglers. Those of us who dote on trout and salmon are now dreaming of mayfly hatches and rushing waters. If only in retrospect, I'll fish tonight.

Anyone can do it, and no laws are broken. You simply sweep a desk clear of workaday tools, install a fly-tying vise and revel in the business of preparing miniature feather lures for a new season.

It has been said that angling is three parts anticipation and one part participation. That's a strong brew, but one's imagination certainly races while artificial flies take shape in a home workshop. Each pattern conjures up old triumphs and immaculate memories. Adventure and tradition are woven into the floss and ribbing, the exotic feathers and the hair of each tiny lure.

Did an old boy named Rube Wood actually design his fly on a stream's bank, copying a natural insect? Whether or not, this is an ancient standard, one of the magic names. There are so many others:

Queen of Waters, Royal Coachman, Gold-ribbed Hare's Ear! To a trout fisherman each is a bugle note sounded through the shimmering green of springtime. Does the handsome red, white and yellow Parmachene Belle really simulate a brook trout's pectoral fin?

No matter, one ties to pattern—because pattern has been successful. As the busy thread circles each quill and feather, each end of tinsel and fraction of peacock herl, the years roll back and a night in March becomes a great day on lake or stream.

Once, too many years ago, Arnold Laine, Bob Williams and I flew into a postage-stamp lake in northern Maine. There, to simulate a nymph found in the gullet of a lusty squaretail trout, we tied a fly of hemp rope and tan calftail. It was deadly enough to slaughter brookies ranging up to more than five pounds, and we called it the Snake Pond Special.

Religiously, year after year, I tie that fly—and it never works the old magic. Still, squinting under the fluorescent lights on an evening in March, there is something vastly satisfying in creating the old patterns.

In central Massachusetts, where I live, no streamer fly collection is complete without a selection of Millers River Specials. The late Henry Scarborough designed this one in the days when most of us counted no season complete without taking an icy plunge at the Bear's Den on the Millers. The rocks were always slippery and each was the size of a bowling ball. Now, thanks to industrial pollution, Bear's Den trout are a memory.

Paul Kukonen, one of the finest trout and salmon fishermen in our north country, added another pattern. Paul, who will tell you about it if you visit him in his Green Street angler's bazaar in Worcester, Massachusetts, noted that the famous Gray Ghost streamer tends to fade and to assume a pink-lavender color after hard use and much exposure to bright sunlight.

Others may have detected the change, but Kukonen—who has an inquiring mind—wondered why the ancient, lavender hued Ghosts seemed more effective than spanking new models. He experimented with dyes and came up with a variation, called the Pink Ghost. It's a fine fly, a killer on landlocked salmon, and it may soon become a standard.

PATTERN, among fly fishermen, should be spelled with capital letters. Innovations may be accepted, but only on a trial basis. It takes years of success before feather merchants accept a new combination of hair, feathers and tinsel. Tradition is a hard taskmaster.

Incurable romantics among trout fishermen are collectors. We delay a deer hunt to visit L. L. Bean's storied emporium at Freeport, Maine, and we emerge with flies that might well have been tied at home. We rarely find it possible to resist some of the nymphs, wets, dries or terrestrials that Kukonen has wheedled out of some obscure genius in Pennsylvania or Michigan. We adore trout flies: we swap them and trade them and place on a special pedestal those created by the hand of a recognized authority.

All trout flies are underpriced. The good ones are difficult to create, and even the worst are the result of hand labor and infinite craftsmanship. You will pay a hefty fee for fine hooks and exotic materials, for skilled tying and exact balance, but you will never appreciate this until you create your own.

Among wet flies I like the March Brown. It's an ancient tidbit, and thoroughly American because it is tied with the webby hackle of a ruffed grouse. Whipping it up, placing the smidgeon of hen pheasant wing, the fur dubbing and the yellow ribbing, one can almost sense the interest of trout in a lure so thoroughly buggy and natural.

My March Browns are tied with grouse feathers downed by my gun, and that makes all the difference! Just as the Cahills that, hopefully, will raise trout in late April and May boast the fine, barred wood duck feathers from a bird that came to me in a red November dawn. You can't buy these feathers, for this is against the law—but you can acquire them legally if you're a hunter.

Certainly this is part and parcel of the delight in tying flies for personal use: each is a delicate masterpiece, into which is woven the utter witchcraft of adventure and triumph. Each is a patchwork classic of materials and memories, of ancient tradition and the strange egotism that possesses proud hunters and fishers.

I tell you there is nothing like a quiet evening hour in March, when a fly takes shape under the circling thread—unless it is that climactic moment when a worthy trout or salmon rises to take a lure that you have fashioned with your own hand.

To All Dogs

Dogs are smelly and they shed hair on expensive rugs, but they get to be part of the family and you tend to forget their obvious transgressions. If a man wants to be sticky about it, kids are smelly too, and they smear peanut butter on the walls. I don't hear much about leash laws for kids, although it might be a good thought.

Once upon a time my sister-in-law, *sans* dog, thought the world had ended when my dachshund gave her sprouts a big, wet kiss. She conjured up germs galore and she hustled those kids out of range.

Now, of course, she has a dog of her own. That mutt not only anoints the children with a long, pink tongue–it sleeps with them. Cindy, or "Syndicate," as I call her to maintain my reputation as a troublesome uncle, is a lovely German short-hair.

Early-on, Cindy had a habit of snatching caps off people's heads. She tried it with me and I belted her across the muzzle. She sat back, wondering if I could be for real, and my sister-in-law also sat back–torn between screaming and slipping a few drops of cyanide into my next highball.

Cindy tried again, and I belted her again. Thereafter, she knew that this particular old character would not stand for the snatching of a cap off a head. Nowadays we are fast friends, but she knows where fun begins and ends. Dogs are smart people.

I hunt with a gentleman named Paul Belton. He owns a Labrador retriever named Blackie, and Blackie is 100 pounds of bone, muscle and sharp, white teeth. A very gentle dog, if you know him, but don't burst into Paul's home unannounced and unknown. That S.O.B. (no profanity intended, for all male dogs are that) would take an arm off at the shoulder.

Therefore I took a calculated risk when I barged in recently. Blackie charged and I noted the horrified expression on the face of Paul's wife: she thought the Lab was going to separate my parts.

Fortunately, Blackie had recognized me and he was bent on extending welcome. Simultaneously, his big forepaws hit my chest and his long, red tongue slopped me from chin to eyebrows. Maybe he thought we were going hunting again.

For some people dogs are necessary. Kids lose much of the magic in life if they do not own a succession of mutts. Hunters forever search for the perfect gun dog, and old timers count themselves very fortunate if one in a lifetime proves ideal.

Few really live up to their masters' boasts, but it is quite unforgivable to criticize a partner's dog. The beast may be a true crocodile, prone to flush birds far out of range or to swallow them whole when downed, but his owner will invent excuses for each breach of discipline.

You can buy a dog for much coin of the realm, complete with pedigree and diploma from a handler, or you can pick up a waif at the Animal Rescue League for a couple or three bucks. Either way, some gamble is involved. Dogs are like humans: some are smart, and some never learn. Many are immaculately clean and others insist on rolling in whatever smells like a body-snatcher's reject.

Traditionally, springtime is the ideal season to acquire a puppy. A hunter or bench show fancier will choose with great care, paying much attention to pedigree and bone structure. The average home-owner probably demands something "cute and cuddly." No matter, in the end of it all hands deal with the intangibles of hope and love.

That's really enough. You acquire a pup and pay for the necessary innoculations. You despair of housebreaking the little rascal until, suddenly, he learns to whine at the door when Nature calls. You work with him, wrestle with him—and pray that he'll be the greatest. He will be!

Every dog becomes a member of the family, for better or for worse. You learn to love each of them for their individuality and their skills, and you characteristically discount their transgressions. You are a zealous press agent for your dog.

I don't see anything wrong with this. All of my dogs have been nonpareils. Weren't yours?

The Time Clock

When a neighbor mentioned that he had seen a woodchuck scurry across a country road, I privately chalked up a case of mistaken identity. After all, it was the second week of March and our northern fields were still snowcovered.

Then, within a few days, two other friends mentioned similar sightings. One of these observers was a highly trained game biologist who was unlikely to mistake a scuttling cottontail for a 'chuck.

Now, in spite of harmless folklore, our northern groundhog does not emerge on February 2 to search for his shadow. Woodchucks are true hibernators, spending the cold weather months in a trance so deep it is the next thing to death.

Woodchucks are vegetarians, as many a back-yard gardener has discovered to his sorrow. These roly-poly burghers of the meadows feast on a surprising variety of green things. Therefore, I had always assumed that the groundhog remained in his earthen quarters until the first shoots of new grass and clover offered topside sustenance. Had something unforseen occurred?

Probably not, for Nature makes few mistakes and the 'chuck is admirably suited to survive in an environment that, for half of the year, is alien to its summer-loving talents. The answers are there, if we can find them.

Groundhogs are gluttons during the warm weather months. They become fat on the largess of summer, and it's this extra fuel that keeps a flickering spark of life burning during a long northern winter.

By late fall woodchucks become progressively lethargic. Finally they seek out deep burrows to enter hibernation well below the frost line. If, during some wintertime excavation, you uncover a groundhog it will be limp and apparently unconscious. Suspended animation is the right term, for a hibernating 'chuck's temperature will dip as low as 37 degrees. The heartbeat is slowed from a normal summer rate of 80 a minute to about four or five.

It seems reasonable to assume that awakening is triggered by the rising temperatures of springtime. Certainly exposure to heat will bring a winter-limp 'chuck back to the land of the living within six or eight hours.

Whether this interruption of natural hibernation has any adverse effect on the animal is anybody's guess. The only one I ever awakened was quick to scramble into a burrow when released. Did he promptly return to the Land of Nod?

I think so, and I'm inclined to believe that the woodchuck seen in early March may well catnap for another month. The truly astonishing thing is the act of emergence while our earth is still frozen and springtime is future tense.

Evidently there is nothing unusual about this, but three groundhogs triggered a good deal of lunch-hour conversation among several of us who are capable of becoming excited about natural phenomena.

Could rising temperatures, in March, have sent a wave of relatively warm air into a frozen burrow? Unlikely. Could a change in light intensity prompt response? Again, doubtful, because wintering 'chucks are far underground.

Instinct is a tough word to define, so why not rely on another force which has yet to be explained by naturalists? It's the biological time clock which somehow tells a bird or mammal that this is the hour to migrate or to do something equally strange.

Very soon now, woodcock will come streaming up the ancient flyways into our cold north country. The gnome-like little timberdoodle feeds on earthworms, yet there'll be no squirmers available when this migrant arrives to claim singing grounds during the frigid month of March.

Nonetheless, away down in Louisiana, something in this curious little game bird's physiological printed circuit has clicked–and the bird goes north.

Light intensity may well be the triggering force that sends an avalanche of birds streaming northward in springtime, but why so very early–before natural food is available? Until the earth warms, a timberdoodle must fast and live on its fat. A woodchuck, emerging at this time of year, must do the same.

I think it obvious that a groundhog is blessed with one of those built-in time clocks. Sometime, long before the surrounding earth melts and green shoots appear, there is a jog in the circuit, a message to increase basic metabolism and come alive.

If a 'chuck could reason–a doubtful possibility in any sense other than dim awareness and natural guile–he might be stunned to emerge into a world still cloaked in ice and snow, with no goodies to feast upon.

Almost fully awake in this tag end of winter, I think he dives back into the chamber that has served him since the first of fall's line storms, to slumber fitfully and to make periodic reconnaissances until the promise of spring is fulfilled.

Are human beings blessed with biological time clocks? Nonsense.

Make the most of it if I have an uncontrollable desire to tie trout flies in March.

The Bells of Springtime

Springtime is never a sudden thing in our north country: it seeps into a man's consciousness in fragmentary glimpses: a high flying wedge of geese against the sky, pussy willows and swelling red maple buds, the unmistakable tinkle of water beneath a gray counterpane of weary frost crystals.

Then the wind returns full force, temperatures plummet and snow squalls fight a rear guard action for the dying winter. I always despair of a new season during these fitful days of March—until that magical night when the first hylas lift their thin voices to the cold stars.

The hyla is a tree frog, best known to outdoorsmen as the spring peeper. He is an atom of life, so small that it would take 300 of his kind to balance a pound weight. Insignificant? Perhaps, and yet I know a lot of hairy-chested sportsmen who pay regular annual courtesy calls upon the hylas.

All winter long these mites of the woodlands have been slumbering under the leaf mold. Now, as melting snow and vernal rains send freshets into the bottom lands, the peepers awaken from their long sleep. Instinctively, a few at first, and then a veritable torrent of tiny bodies, they seek out the pools and marshes which will serve as nuptial bowers.

Long ago some incurable romantic among that usually far from flighty breed of men called biologists spoke of the hylas' chorus as "the bells of springtime." Heard from a distance, the thin, multitudinous voices of the spring peepers actually sound like elfin sleigh bells. H. G. Tapply, an old friend and fellow worker in the vineyards of outdoor writing, calls them "pinkletinks." By any name, this is a lovely sound.

Perhaps, on the first night of our annual symphony, only a few clear, thin notes will be heard. Each seems tuned to an individual pitch, but each is almost bell-like in clarity and quality of tone. Only the males lift their voices in song: females, apparently, are good listeners.

Attuned to the treacherous Ides of March, spring peepers will serenade their sweethearts when 30-degree temperature is etching ice crystals across a marsh—but below that reading the singers stand mute.

It is probably enough to park one's car at the edge of a woodsy pool to listen, strangely satisfied, to this exultant chorus—but I have an insatiable curiosity. Therefore, each year, there is one night in which I choose to renew old acquaintances at close quarters. It isn't easy.

Hylas resent an unfamiliar noise or presence. If your booted foot snaps a twig or splashes water, nearby voices cease. Then you stand, like some patient old night heron in the dark, waiting. And, since there is an urgency burning in the peepers—or more prosaically they have short memories—the voices soon resume.

Now another cautious step—and another—until you have pinpointed one atom of life by the sound of his reedy voice raised among the multitudes. *Now?*

If the sudden flashlight's beam is well directed, he'll be there—a sleek, impossibly small olive-gray frog with a dark cross on his back and a transparent bubble at his throat. Often the hyla will be in the water or perched on a hummock. Sometimes I find them well up in a tangle of brush.

Caught in the unmerciful light, a spring peeper freezes, the round bagpipe of his throat still extended. If you scoop him up you'll find that each miniature foot is equipped with sucker-disced toes, the better to climb trees where he'll forage for insects all summer long.

Nobody looks for hylas in July, but right now there is something immeasurably satisfying about the bells of springtime.

First Encounter

On this deceptively mild morning the sun defeated a low cloud cover and, for a wonderful moment, springtime seemed a distinct possibility. Since our northern fishing seasons get under way in April, I thought it wise to prospect. Others, it developed, had the same idea.

Without some inner glow of anticipation, this sort of thing might well be an exercise in frustration. Fortunately, every trout fisherman lives in the future. If the air is raw and cold, with a wind right out of the Devil's refrigerator, we dream of warmth and burgeoning green leaves, of handsome squaretails rising to gauzy-winged mayflies.

The clues are scant enough. I came to a wooden bridge which spans a suburban stream. A phoebe darted out of cover at my approach. Later, this happy little gray gnome of a bird would build a nest among the bridge supports, over the singing stream.

There were tired drifts of gray snow in the black growth, a reminder of wintertime. Ice still rimmed the flood, pearly and jagged where budding willows nodded. Wordlessly, I leaned over the rough-planked railing and searched for life.

Nothing is quite like running water to intrigue an observer, especially the clean gouts of springtime. If that Twentieth Century sickness called pollution is evident in green slime anchored to the once immaculate boulders, winter's anesthesia curbs its spread. At this time of year, if never again, streams approach faultless clarity—all the better for those of us who make pilgrimages.

A fisherman doesn't look at the water, he looks through it. Gradually the currents sort themselves out and a fish becomes apparent—then another! Three shadowy forms were there, just above the stony bottom. They flickered back and forth, holding in the current, changing position as effortlessly as butterflies sampling a field of clover.

Breathlessly—and I have done this for so many years that the action is stereotyped—I found a twig and broke it into tiny bits. Each piece was launched to float serenely in the crystal flood, and each drew the attention of a trout.

Again and again those graceful fish rose, their white-edged fins flashing, to take the proferred bits—and to eject them almost as quickly. They'd never be so trusting when the law allowed a hook imbedded in each tempter.

Away off in the warmth of late May, dreaming of dry flies and fine leader tippets, I never heard the car which arrived. Indeed I hardly glanced at the man who appeared beside me. He had a bottle of pickled salmon eggs, better fare than my twigs.

Bundled against the chill wind, we held that bridge together, silently applauding each trout as it rose to intercept a glowing egg. Eons later, or so it seemed, I recognized my companion as a famed city sportsman who scorns any lure other than a floating artificial. Like me, he was rushing the season.

We weren't alone. Thousands of anglers were out on this raw April weekend, just looking. Unlike the impatient youngsters who come with rod and line and who are warned to cease and desist by gruff game wardens, our operation fed the soul rather than the creel.

At that time it was more than enough to see trout holding against clean currents, to see the flush of red in maple buds, to hear a grackle and see black ducks volplaning over marshlands so recently locked in snow and ice.

Just possibly no moment in time or space would ever hold so great a measure of magic. We launch a new season on our own terms, envisioning something so delightful that it cannot materialize.

Or maybe it has, here and now, with a vision superimposed over mud and melting snow and a wind that sieves winter-weary flesh.

The observers of trout are dreamers, and who cares to challenge a dream?

So Heady a Brew

If you are fond of old saws and you live in central New England, it is quite right to believe that April showers bring mayflowers—even if sunshine and sudden warmth are more important than the cold rain of this fourth month.

On the other hand, northern Maine, New Hampshire and Vermont may not boast this most fragile of blossoms until Memorial Day. That's because mayflowers are attuned to the advancing equinox; they flower when snow disappears and sudden heat pierces last year's fallen leaves.

This plant is an elfin thing of the aboriginal north woods, flourishing in sandy, secret places—languishing where our cement civilization devours the wilderness. Arbutus has a poor opinion of mankind.

In central and southern New England at this time of year, and especially along the sand-bordered roads of Cape Cod, small boys stand at the roadside, grimy fists clutching bundles of delicate pink bloom—yours for a silver coin. To me, this transaction is sacrilege.

Wildflowers are precious, hence they should be diverted from the channels of commerce, even where boys are concerned. The mayflower is never so great a prize as when it is encountered during a sentimental journey into spring woodlands.

You go when sunlight blesses the ridges, when pussy willows are butter yellow with pollen and the first flush of red maples washes a valley with crimson. Snow may fight a rear guard action in the black growth—and it may snow tonight—but now the earth virtually steams and migrating warblers twitter as they journey northward.

It is much too late for hunting, and too early to fish for trout. Like an old hermit of the woodlands you shuffle through last year's leaves, unarmed and strangely content. There is always a south slope where the sun is a benediction and the partridges take their ease. When a deer rocks off, you think of late fall and powder smoke, but the thought is incongruous. April and May are months of renewal. There is perfume in the air.

This scent is a medley of vague aromas: it is the flowing sap of sugar maples, the clean pungence of skunk cabbages, of pollen from a myriad of early blooming shrubs and weeds. It is all of these things and more, mingling with the heavy, sweet-and-rotten musk of leaf mold deteriorating under the combined guns of frost and moisture and sudden, incubating warmth.

Best of all, among springtime perfumes, is a thin stream of fragrance which, once sampled, is never forgotten. For those of us who call New England home, no flower exudes so heady a brew, and none is so retiring as the arbutus. It might well be argued that Yankees are prejudiced, that the mayflower's reputation far exceeds its physical self. Perhaps this is so, but I am prepared to argue the point.

I know that there is something immensely satisfying in trudging the woodlands at this time of year, in raking the dead stuff of an ancient fall season away from a hint of concealed, dull green leaves, and in discovering those tiny pink and white bell flowers that waft a well-remembered fragrance into the mixing bowl of spring.

Granted, mayflowers are individually tiny, their colors pale, more than anything in Nature all virginal pink and white. If there is such a thing as perfection in miniature, here is an example.

The scent of arbutus is quite as retiring as the plant's nature. Nearby, this fragrance is delightfully robust and pleasing, yet it never pervades an entire section of woodland or swamp, cloying one's senses as azalea does in June.

Because mayflowers are still plentiful in New England, yet hidden from those who do not know where to look, they will probably endure until the cement and steel arteries of "progress" over-run our land.

Unfortunately, a few well-meaning but ignorant citizens annually decimate the arbutus: they rip this fragile plant from the earth,
thus destroying it forever. Old woodsmen harvest a minimum of
blooms, clipping stems close to earth, so that the creeping rootlets
may endure. A sharp knife is essential if you would collect a small
treasure of these classic blossoms.

Some say that no mayflower should be taken from the woods. I
do not agree, but then–I'm a hunter and a fisherman. Those of us
who swear by rod and gun sport are charlatans of the first order. We
tend to make bad jokes about Nature lovers–and we prove to be the
gentlest of earth's admirers. We shoot game birds during a short
season, and then spend the rest of the year aiding our quarry. We
are latter-day savages with a fishing rod, but we replace more trout
than we take.

In April and May a hard-eyed deer hunter collects arbutus for his
bride, and for himself. A fisherman will leave feeding squaretails to
reconnoiter a slope where mayflowers bloom.

If arbutus ever needs a friend in New England, rest assured that
the first offer of help will come from a man behind a rod and gun.

Anglers Are Dreamers

Those of us who place trout fishing somewhere close to family ties and love of country find it difficult to explain an almost psychotic desire to wade cold streams in a northern springtime. Of course one may blame it on the fish. I have spent so many sleepless nights prior to an opening day, and always the thought of great trout was in my mind—huge squaretails, rising out of the depths of dreams.

Come to think of it, early trout fishing must be reserved for dreamers, and not for scientific anglers. At this point waters are still frigid and the fish logy. Insect hatches are almost nonexistent. Things will be much better in another month, but—mark you—things will never be precisely the same.

April anglers dress like December deer hunters, for the east wind can be sharp. Nonetheless, a fisherman savors that pale hour of dawn when the first robins, all fluffed up to ward off the chill, salute another springtime. Later, after sunrise, there'll be a steady background twitter, the lisping notes of tiny warblers hurrying northward and gossiping as they go.

Perhaps, given a bit of luck, one may even pause to smile at the erratic motorcylce beat of an old cock grouse drumming on a fallen log. His wings are the bongo drums of springtime and he is the very spirit of the northern wilderness which so often seems to be threatened by industry and suburban sprawl.

If the trees are bare in this mid-watch of April, surely they are on a threshold. The wash of color—red with a hint of gold—speaks of leaves about to reject the dormant cocoon of winter. There is a swelling of buds against the sky.

Anglers are dreamers, so one cannot fault them for pausing to check a slope carpeted with mayflowers. First of the floral legions, prospering under a pall of dead leaves, these tiny, delicate pink and white blossoms waft a heady perfume into the warming air. Few outdoorsmen will admit as much, but perfume is a great thing in the April woodlands: it is a subtle blend, a trace of the first, hidden flowers, of sap flowing and trees budding, of skunk cabbages in the marshes.

If streams are running over their banks and crystals of ice still clutch at quiet pools, one must be excused for spending too much time studying the sharply etched tracks of a deer in bankside mud, or the hummock where an otter dined on the sucker that followed an April moon up a strident watercourse to spawn.

Any angler who is worthy of his salt returns to well remembered places, perhaps to see whether watercress is still growing in a certain run, whether the woodcock have returned to an ancient singing ground, to visit a beaver dam and inspect the meticulous work of the paddle-tailed engineers.

Obviously, there is a great deal of departmentalized research in this early fishing. Who but an angler, clumsy in hip boots or waders, would trudge over a laurel ridge to determine the survival of porcupines in a tumbled ledge? Who else to audition the white-throated sparrow's song and to attest that the "little sweet-voice" of Indian legend still heralds a northern springtime?

In April, in our north country, fishing may be poor. Still, the dream is there—plus so many delightful options. If, incredibly, a handsome native trout rises to the fly, takes, is hooked, played and brought to net as precious as the Holy Grail, then mid-April may indeed challenge the flower-time of May.

Much Magic

Once in a blue moon all of the imponderables click into place and a morning measures up to the standards we boast in our northern Chamber of Commerce brochures. So immaculate a day should not be squandered in gainful labor.

I had showered and shaved and arrayed myself in the sharply pressed uniform of an office-bound lackey when some perfume off the back forty, or maybe some snatch of birdsong called a halt. Is there any reason why an adult cannot play hookey?

It was still too early for apple blossoms, yet a faint flush of pink suffused the ancient Baldwin at the foot of our lawn. The wild cherries were bursting their buds and marsh marigolds gilded a nearby swamp. Before the sun was well up robins were caroling and the nearby hills seemed to squirm with heat ghosts. I chose to go fishing.

There is a stream in my bailiwick, a lovely little feeder that winds through a succession of sleepy little towns. Those of us who love trout like to believe that native squaretails dart through its quiet pools and runs, yet we know that most of the fish are recently stocked. Perhaps it doesn't matter.

I arrived on a weekday when most of my neighbors were busily employed elsewhere. The kids were still in school, so the banks of this creek were deserted by mankind. Adjusting a slightly cockeyed halo–since I smoke a pipe–I retrieved two empty cigarette packets and stuck them in my coat for later burning in an incinerator. Litter is an abomination on a wilderness stream.

A pair of wood ducks spoiled the first pool, spattering out and squealing after the manner of their kind. The drake towered, reversed his course and then bored close overhead. He'd have been an easy shot in November, and I pointed the fly rod. Ducks like solitude, so I had to be the first interloper on this sunny morning.

It was perfect, all the way from the redwinged blackbirds teetering on green willows to a hatch of gauzy-winged flies which I assumed were *Iron fraudator,* the first of the legions. Clear water rushed out of a shallow run and poured into a deep, black hole. Long before I saw widening rings, I heard the slurping rise of a good trout at the head of the pool.

He was feeding steadily, rising to take those delicate flies. My fingers were clumsy in attaching a sparse Quill Gordon to the 4X leader tippet. That fish was all of a foot long, and I wanted him in the worst kind of a way!

Fortunately, there was ample room for a back cast and no wind to deflect the offering. I always cast well when no one is looking, and this fly dropped perfectly, some four feet ahead of the feeding trout. Breathlessly, mending the line, I waited as my Quill Gordon rode the current nicely cocked–and then disappeared in a dimple of swirling water.

No trout is quite so precious as the first of a season taken on a dry fly. This was a rainbow, obviously no native—but a plump and handsome little battler. He came clear in three successive jumps, and then the slim glass rod had its way. I shook the miniature hook free and let him go.

It was that way all morning, a succession of pools and runs, each populated by gleaming little trout. There were grouse drumming on nearby hillsides and warblers lisping in the alders. The sunlight was impossibly warm and the earth sent up a flowery aroma.

Later, having absorbed much magic, I cranked up and went home. A neighbor asked–what luck? And I came mighty close to explaining. Just caught myself in the nick of time.

He would have raised an eyebrow at the release of every trout. Having never fished, he'd have thought me very odd to exult about a brace of wood ducks, grouse on a hillside, warblers inching their way northward—and the absolute perfection of a morning in the sunshine and shadow of a small stream.

"Didn't catch a thing," I grinned. "That's fishing!"

The Prospectors

When I was a sprout, and this is a long cast back, supposedly literate teenagers submitted prose and poetry to a magazine called *St. Nicholas.* "What Really Happened" was, as I recall, one basic theme for development.

I thought of it the other day when a friend of mine told me how he and his wife made a Sunday morning trip through the awakening countryside. Will Sanders is a sportsman and a gone goose about the joys of pheasant hunting. What really happened on this morning in May? I can guess.

First off, the sun was warm and all of the landscape was clothed in a lace of new green. Occasional apple trees were in full bloom, while others displayed pink buds in a speckled heaven of emerging leaves. Everywhere birds were singing and wheeling through the treetops.

We humans have too few mornings in May, hence Will and Rose Sanders were captivated—but for different reasons. When Sanders parked his car beside an old apple orchard bordered by an immense swale swamp, his good wife was entranced by the idyllic explosion of leaf and blossom.

Will made noises which indicated similar pleasure, but he puffed a battered pipe more rapidly than usual, and his eyes had narrowed. Obviously, the big swale curving around an overgrown orchard indicated prime habitat for ringnecked pheasants. Sanders duly noted a scrub oak hillside and a distant slope that might well be planted to corn.

Rose was luxuriating in May, but Will had projected himself into a future October, with the swale gone sere and windfalls glowing like rubies under those huddled trees. It was a spot to remember when a new hunting season got under way.

Will Sanders is far from unique. Upland hunters, almost to a man, pursue their sport in every season. Granted, the guns are cased during nine months of the wheeling year, but we all evaluate covers. (In hunting season there is a corresponding need to peer into trout brooks and to exult about the darting forms of squaretails seeking sanctuary.)

I happen to be a nut on ruffed grouse and woodcock, hence every spring fishing expedition is improved by the sound of a drumming partridge or the timberdoodle that twitters out of streamside alders. Is it not possible that these magnificent game birds will sire phalanxes of their kind for the guns of November?

Therefore Sanders becomes thoughtful while he reconnoiters big swales and orchard edges, corn fields and the tangled brush of remote truck gardens. I climb into a mental time machine when springtime prospecting turns up new alder runs and forgotten farmsites where the wild apple trees exhibit their pink and white blooms in a framework of white birches.

Grouse will gravitate to good cover, and good cover means natural foodstuffs—such as worm-riddled wild apples and aspen buds. If there is a stream trickling down, occasional conifers for shelter, a swamp-edge stippled with alders and a few slopes which boast the anemic gleam of poplar, there is no mistake. Grouse will be there, and so will I—with a light scattergun six months hence.

Water is quite as instructive. I know men who interrupt tall tales about fishing with breathless asides about the ducks flushed in a great marsh. In springtime the squealing woodies and erudite blacks are there, obviously setting up housekeeping. Gunners are creation's foremost conservationists in May, yet at this time of the year we exhibit the sunny side of a dual personality.

Usually, anticipation is sweeter than any actual harvest. Indeed, I have a sneaking suspicion that we hunters and fishers derive as much joy in planning our adventures as we do in their consummation. Tomorrow is forever bright and successful, hence we live for tomorrow.

That's what really happens.

Melody in the Night

Life is much too short to lose any part of May, so I am thinking of taking a sabbatical. Anyone who languishes in a city office while the north country turns green is, at the very least, ill advised.

This is a time to recharge the batteries of life. It is not enough to note the gold of blossoming Norway maples dripping into a superhighway, or to comment on the sudden wash of fresh color that mists a hardwood ridge. One must participate.

When I was young, and consequently in love with a succession of delightful nymphets, the whippoorwill was a good excuse to seek some country lane, to park and to listen–to explore the wisdom of Freud and Audubon.

I hope that today's young people are similarly impressed. The grand symphony of Nature encompasses all of us. History repeats, but the earth never changes. Under the wheeling constellations the boy I used to be, so many years ago, is mirrored in the lad of today.

Admittedly, I am changed–by war and time and circumstance–but the man who came here as a beardless boy still hears the same immortal strain, a whippoorwill pouring his heart out upon a moon-drenched wilderness. There is, as always there has been, the majesty of night itself–the warm, dark velvet cloak of May where huge, bespangled night moths dance away their one week span of life.

There was, and is, the glint of living water and the glimmer of low-hanging stars to tell us that the time is *now!*

You simply go where a silver lake reflects everything on earth and in the heavens, where the black growth casts shadows too deep for penetration. You go where the grating sound of industry is a murmur under the far horizon.

Then, having parked your atomic age motor vehicle and waited for the alien echoes of the internal combustion engine to fade away, you hear it at last—the clean, clear roundelay of a whippoorwill. There is nothing so stirring in our nearby wilderness, no sound so completely melodious, incisive and wild.

Curiously, while the whippoorwill must be counted among best known northern birds, it is probably least often seen. It is, for all practical purposes, a disembodied voice—a lyrical melody in the deep night.

If, having the patience and the skill of an old hunter, you find one of our Yankee poltergeists, it will be squatting among the dead leaves in thick underbrush, or perched horizontally on a low tree limb. The bird does not fly in bright sunlight, and its black-brown-buff feather pattern is an armor of magnificent camouflage.

Backwoods motorists sometimes see whippoorwills for brief moments, pinned in the merciless glare of headlights which sweep a dirt road. Then there is a fragmentary impression of ruby-red, glowing eyes before soft wings flutter and the bird disappears.

This is one of a group called goatsuckers, for no good reason other than the superstition of ancient man. Our antecedents saw these spirits of the dusk and darkness flying among their herds, and immediately assumed that the birds were suckling goats!

All of this retiring family, the whippoorwill, the poor will, the chuck-will's-widow and the night hawk, are insect eaters. They are equipped with wide, whisker-fringed mouths which have become adapted to the capture of bugs in full flight.

Therefore, whenever a night hawk or a whippoorwill is discovered weaving over and around a herd of sleepy cattle—or goats—be assured that the bird is decimating insect hordes. That's its sole mission on earth.

For a small fraction of life—rarely measuring more than ten inches from inferior beak to tail—the whippoorwill boasts a remarkably loud voice and amazing stamina. Birders have counted more than

1,000 successive calls without a pause, each as strong and clear as the first.

Often several whippoorwills will serenade the nighttime in one given area, and researchers have determined that there is a subtle difference in the well recognized melody. Some of the soloists are more accomplished than others. Is this an end product of practice which distinguishes older birds? Or, may one simply assume that, like human beings, some whippoorwills are blessed with finer voices than others? Nobody really knows.

Then, of course, there is the fourth note.

That clear, penetrating three syllable melody is almost always preceded by a low, vibrant "chuck." You'll have to stalk within a few yards to hear it, but it's there. And then, if you're lucky—or perhaps skillful enough to attain a point where binoculars can be focussed on a calling bird, you'll see him make a quick little curtsy or bow as each individual note is uttered.

Our whippoorwill bows to the ecstasy of a warm, spring night, to his waiting mate—to a time of awakening and renewal in the flowering northland. I see no time wasted, and no incongruity, in deserting human endeavors to spend a few quiet hours appreciating the annual concert.

In addition to lads and lasses who may have other reasons for attending, I tell you that a lot of gnarled, ancient and burly outdoorsmen will salute the arrival of springtime by lending an attentive ear to the bird that sings each night away.

Nightcrawler Time

I had forgotten all about a once popular sport, and then young Billy Michalak, who lives across the street, arrived on a rainy evening in May to borrow a flashlight.

"For what?" I growled–and knew before he had time to answer. The nightcrawlers would be out. No country boy ever buys fish bait when he can harvest a good supply on a wet night.

Billy wangled lend-lease of a flashlight, and I tried to put the whole business out of mind. There wasn't a chance, in spite of a story deadline. Seduced by the rush of warm rain on my windows, I found another flashlight and left the office. It was high time to research an old art, to see whether memory plays tricks.

Although scorned by purists who swear by delicate, feather-dressed artificials, nightcrawlers are prime fish baits. The squirmers probably catch more trout, perch and bass than all of our sophisticated lures combined.

I am no puritan; indeed I often enjoy a morning of worming a small stream where fly casting is impossible. Much skill is involved in this operation, a fact studiously ignored by some status-minded anglers who would like to believe that a fly is the ultimate weapon.

Wormers are legion, so they range from the schoolboy and duffer up to exceptionally talented practitioners. You have, first, a multitude of beginners who are convinced that worms and nightcrawlers are the greatest of all baits to lure a fish. Then, like fine gold lacing plebeian gravel, there are experts. I know a man who has mastered just about every outdoor art, yet he uses fine strips or fillets of worm on miniature hooks to murder trout.

Whatever the technique, an angler must first procure his bait. You can dig in an erstwhile tomato patch, garden or chicken run. Or, you can capture nightcrawlers on the surface during any spring night when rain is falling or a heavy dew has moistened the ground.

I opt for night work, if only because it insures a separate adventure. Catching nightcrawlers is sport in itself, far removed from angling. A measure of skill is involved.

On this evening in May I wanted no can of bait for fishing. Nightcrawlers hopefully harvested would be donated to my youthful friend across the street. My sortie was sport, nothing more.

But, sport with a vengeance! The collecting of nightcrawlers can be adventure in itself. Never question spots of light creeping across a golf course or park in the deep night. Anglers are seeking bait.

Some say that a flashlight which is fitted with a red lens is most effective. I have never found it so, and I use plain, old-fashioned white light. Even with this it is difficult to spot a nightcrawler stretched out on the ground, enjoying a midnight shower.

Since we are creatures of tradition, I hold that no receptacle matches a large, empty tomato tin. Toss a handful of loam in the bottom of this can and you are ready. Use a king-sized container. A man admits defeat if he goes into combat armed with a tiny vessel.

The ease with which nightcrawlers can be gathered will depend, naturally, upon their abundance and–more important–on the amount of rainfall. A real gully-washer will bring them out in force, while a fine mist or dew insures more difficult hunting.

With the exception of flood conditions–a worm-gatherer's dream because nightcrawlers will be right on the surface–you will find most of the squirmers halfway out and halfway in. Harvesting undamaged bait then depends upon tactics.

An earthworm is one of nature's simple creatures, yet it responds to both light and vibration. Tread softly when you seek garden hackle at night, else your quarry will vanish. Move quickly when the probing light discloses one half, say, of a nightcrawler on the surface.

I will not go into the books to find out why it is so, but a crawler halfway in and halfway out of the ground is completely relaxed. If you can grab the head end of this critter quickly and, almost in the same instant, snatch it out of the ground, the worm will not be able to expand its caboose and resist capture.

Snatch quickly and surely. If you botch the procedure, the worm will either escape or will be broken into two pieces. Either way, you lack effective fish bait. Success depends upon split-second coordination.

Small boys are quick to learn. Professors of zoology take longer, probably because they spend too much time studying the sensory organs of a nightcrawler instead of attending to the business at hand.

I'm a nut on fly casting for trout, yet there's much to be said for worm gathering on a wet, warm and muddy night in springtime. Why let kids enjoy all of the fun in life?

Low Key Delight

Sometimes there's a morning when everything falls in place as naturally as a sequence in a daydream. This was one of them.

At 8 a.m. my north country lake resembled a Japanese print. There was no wind and a low mist carpeted the pollen-speckled water.

I traveled at full bore, standing erect in the sternsheets, feeling my little aluminum boat buoyed up as though it moved through air. Behind me the wake frothed, subsided and became a wide vee of profane ripples. It was good to be alone in a world of quiet water and late spring warmth.

Yesterday this boat had battered offshore rips at the tip of Cape Cod. The wind was keening, then, and a vicious chop abetted heavy ground swells. Big pollock swarmed in the rips and it was fury all the way.

That, of course, is one of the major differences between inland and coastal angling. There is elemental struggle in the salt chuck, always a sense of high adventure which is spiced with peril. I'm fond of the sensation.

And yet I'm also fond of a quiet morning on an inland lake. No great gamesters are there, no tidal rips and bursting offshore bars—no ground swells or line squalls to make life hectic. A pair of black

ducks spattered away as I banked into a quiet bay where willows were impossibly green above the thin surface mist.

A flat-bottomed rowboat was anchored just above a spot I'd hoped to fish. Quickly, I cut the gun and ghosted along. A man and a boy waved cheerfully, relieved to find that their morning paradise was invaded by another angler, rather than a hot-rod outboarder.

There was plenty of room. My outboard puttered softly and the tin boat crept ahead. Finally, at a point where willows bowed and weed beds were obvious in eight feet of clear water, I drifted and lowered a mushroom anchor. The ripples widened, flattened and disappeared.

Somewhere a radio sent pop music across the lake. It was a muted sound, a background melody for tranquility. The boy in the nearby boat whispered exultantly as he winched a bluegill aboard. Somehow he seemed to feel that shouting would mar the bright morning, and I saw his father smile indulgently. They were using angleworms and bobbers.

My rod was a new 2½-ounce fiberglass Hardy. Planning a trip to Wyoming's Snake River, I'd purchased this wand hours earlier. Perhaps it would wrestle a rainbow from the shade of the Grand Tetons, but now its mission was less exotic. I wanted calico bass and bluegills.

Both are plentiful in our northern waters, and either will take a fly with the greatest abandon. Suddenly yesterday's big pollock were forgotten. I had some trouble tying a miniature red and white fly to the leader's tippet.

Perhaps some psychologist can explain why an angler can be just as excited about a panfish as a record tuna. I've seen some of the world's great fishermen in action and, like you and me, they get just as shaken and happy when seeking the smaller gamesters as the monsters of the sea.

In this lake the water was very clear, so I could see the fly as it touched down and began to sink. A bluegill darted up out of the weeds and flashed its red-orange flanks. The line tightened, and I was on. First cast!

The boy whispered sibilantly as I brought this saucer-sized quarry to boat, flicked the hook clear and let it go back. Grackles sailed along the bank. The shoreside radio unaccountably rendered Bing Crosby's "White Christmas." We fished in blessed peace.

Blue gills predominated. They seemed never-ending, and yet

twice I saw the pale, ghostly shape of a calico bass rise out of the weeds. Finally, delighted with the bluegills, yet weary of catching them on every cast, I switched to a quick-sinking line.

Now the fly dropped swiftly and I watched as a calico bass finned up out of concealing bottom cover. He came deliberately, sculling along in pursuit of the tiny feather lure, and he looked very big and pale against the dark bottom.

Excited, yet recalling many similar occasions, I resisted the quick strike as that ghostly fish extended its telescopic jaws, sucked the fly in—and turned. Only then, as the line snugged up, did I lift the tip. He was on.

A calico bass is not a great fighter, but he has a few spectacular tricks to exhibit. This one, true to his kind, turned a wide flank to the line's pull and then spattered across the surface. He looked as big as a dinner plate, and I suspect he was a foot long and half as deep-keeled. I let him go.

Three more came in rapid succession, plus a half-dozen bluegills that insisted upon crashing the gate. It was wonderful fishing, made more delightful when a hen mallard paraded her three ducklings through the shadow and shine of the willows.

The lad in the next boat was pop-eyed. Finally, above the shushing of his dad, he inquired: "Mister, don't you like fish?"

"Love 'em," I said, hauling the anchor and preparing to depart—"so I left 'em all for you!"

He was still shaking his head when I putt-putted out of the cove and then cracked the throttle wide open. That boy was absorbing the wonders of fishing, and he needed trophies to prove his new-found skill. He'd learn.

Who, other than a lad, needs dead fish to prove a great morning on the water?

The Night Flyers

On this morning in late May my *Cecropia* moths were emerging, so I had to call the office and declare that a series of blessed events would delay an appearance. Since I am a long-time bachelor, this announcement drew a throaty chuckle from our receptionist. It was no laughing matter to me.

I'd raised those magnificent night moths from miniscule eggs deposited a full year ago. They'd prospered as caterpillars through high summer, feeding on wild cherry foliage, and had then entombed themselves in cocoons of the purest silk. Now their astonishing life cycle was ending in a grand finale.

Many of the great night moths are single-brooded: that is, their larvae take most of a summer to mature, and then remain in chrysalid form through the winter months. These seldom-seen and most flamboyant flyers boast wingspreads of four to seven inches, and they are beautiful to behold.

A *Cecropia*, for example, is a symphony in glowing maroon and subtle brown, with strange purple eye-markings on forewings and half-moon etchings aft. Anyone with half an imagination can see the spirit of deep night in curious lightning flashes of color and cabalistic designs on soft wings.

This is the end of a cycle, and it is short-lived. One of these huge silk moths emerges from its cocoon to exist for a mere six or seven

61

days. The only function of the adult is to breed and to deposit eggs: it never eats or drinks; it is a very transient delight.

Now, in a wire-meshed cage built to discourage a host of mice, chipmunks, squirrels and birds eager to feed on so delectable an assortment of morsels, my chrysalids were bursting their shells. At 9 a.m. I had seen the spot of moisture at the tips of two cocoons and I had smelled the musky scent of that natural enzyme which the emerging moth uses to open a passage.

They had dared much and they had succeeded against great odds. The caterpillar had to escape hungry birds and squirrels, assorted other beasties and parasitic insects prior to spinning a cocoon. Once ensconced in that casket of close-woven silk, the "green worm" had shrivelled, apparently died, and had then split its skin to appear as a cylindrical pupae.

At no time is the miracle of creation so apparent. The pupae is subtly marked with folded wings and legs and antennae, yet that fragile case is filled with a substance as thin as milk. Given a proper number of cold weather months, followed by the heat of the vernal equinox, the perfect insect is formed.

I stand in awe as this magic develops. The moth hatches on a morning in mid- to late May, usually between 9 and 10 a.m. when the sun is warm. There is, first, the enzyme discharged as a softening agent. It has a wild and aboriginal smell, neither pleasant nor abhorrent.

Then the cocoon trembles. Slowly the moth struggles out of confinement: it is an almost unrecognizable creature, wet, bedraggled and elongated–but it requires this struggle to survive. If you slit a cocoon to aid a moth's emergence, that moth will die. Let Nature take its course.

The limp, moist and limber creature finally frees itself and precariously wraps its uncertain legs around a supporting twig. Initially, a *Cecropia's* wings are very short and crumpled. Swiftly they lengthen, to hang like wet velvet drapes. The beneficent sun beats down and progress is rapid.

Within a half hour those marvelous wings, with all of their rich color and strange markings, attain full length and breadth. The moth pumps them slowly, forcing a hardening liquid through all of the multitudinous struts which internally brace an airfoil. By mid-afternoon this natural creation is as perfect as ever it will be.

Now I have alternatives. I can tether a female by a fine thread tied to a wing strut and leave her on the lawn overnight. Before dawn a male will pay court. Thereafter I can keep the female and gather her eggs to start a whole new dynasty of night moths.

Or I can let her go free. She'll live all of a week, cavorting among the late apple blossoms and new foliage, romancing and depositing her eggs. At the end of this brief period my moth, male or female, will destroy itself in a paroxysm of fluttering suicide.

This year I choose to release all captives. They have given me a small measure of knowledge, plus photographs, plus lots of work in arranging protective nets for caterpillars and in changing pastures when those caterpillars have devoured available forage.

The *Cecropias* will find Nature a far harder taskmaster than Woolner, for they won't have a nylon net to screen them from birds and parasitic insects and murderous insecticides, but they'll be free.

That makes all of the difference.

To Kill a Lake

Curt Gowdy really has nothing to do with this story, aside from posing a question for which there is no ready answer–at least none readily manufactured by a working outdoor writer. Curt, Hal Lyman and I had spent a great day catching sea-run brook trout on a private stream "somewhere on Cape Cod," as the war correspondents used to say. There are two reasons for camouflage: first, the stream is owned and managed by Hal's family; second, it's a tiny creek.

Back at the lodge, after dinner, we were discussing the effect of publicity on a small stream or pond. Gowdy, who is NBC's ace sportscaster, sipped something tinkly, raised his eyebrows and asked: "How can an honest outdoor writer justify killing a lake with publicity?"

He meant, of course, that an exciting newspaper or magazine article about angling on any given body of water is certain to draw the multitudes. Overfishing can ruin peak sport. Therefore, those of us who write about angling sometimes destroy the thing we love best.

The question is fair, and no outdoor scribbler worthy of his salt has failed to wrestle with the problem. We're paid to report on angling and readers deserve a fair shake. Is there a possibility that, by too objective reporting, we also short-change the public?

Make no mistake, the better rod and gun writers use a gimmick. They name the big waters, where over-exploitation is unlikely regardless of promotion, and they use such weasel words as "a stream in northern Washington County" to prevent naming a small creek that could be fished out on a mob weekend.

This is good policy–or utterly unfair– depending upon your point of view. Unfortunately it doesn't solve the problem, for some very big streams and wilderness lakes have been rendered mediocre by crowds vectored in by writers.

Once, long ago, I murdered a pond. Granted, it would have been killed a few years later by lumbermen who coveted an adjacent swamp full of pulp and who therefore drove a logging road to its shores, but I still feel guilty.

It was a little place which glistened like a turquoise in the black growth of Maine's Grand Lake Mattagamon country. Back in 1948 you either packed in, poled a canoe–or flew a bush plane out of Mattagamon or Shinn Pond.

There were no lumber roads to Snake at that time, and no easy access. Even flying was a white knuckle affair, for you had to side-slip in, and spruce trees reached for your laboring propeller on the way out. It was man against the wilderness all the way.

But wilderness has its own compensations. At Snake Pond the squaretail trout grew to astonishing proportions. Two-pounders were commonplace and anyone who failed to catch at least one four or five-pounder had to be a lousy fisherman.

Paul Kukonen, that paragon of central Massachusetts anglers, had been in–and he raved about the trophy brookies that walloped blue maribou streamer flies. Arnold Laine, Bob Williams and I decided to make the trip. It was quite an adventure at that time.

We motored up to Shinn Pond and found a bush pilot named Elmer Wilson, a great guy who–last I heard–was still flying people into remote lakes, only now the virgin ponds are away up in Canada. He agreed to take us in one at a time in his single-engined float plane.

Unlike today's well equipped back-of-beyond sports, we borrowed a horse blanket to use as a tent fly. We stocked up on such staples as bacon and tea and flour and tinned beans.

Arnold growled at anything more than tea and salt: he wanted to live off the land, with trout and fiddleheads a main course. Laine insisted on camping close to a feeder stream where angling was superb. The black flies and mosquitoes feasted, but fishing was the stuff of which dreams are made. And we were young, and we had found an angler's Mecca.

These were squaretails mind you, and they averaged two to three pounds apiece. Every now and then one of us would latch on to a four or five pounder. The blue maribou streamer worked, but we dreamed up a bulky nymph–later dubbed the "Snake Pond Special"–made of hemp rope fiber and a pinch of brown calftail. It was murder incorporated, and I hate to admit that it has never worked elsewhere.

The place seemed to be infested with big, brilliantly colored brook trout. We ate a few. We let most of them go. We hollered at the loons and they shrieked back. There were moose and bear tracks to examine. Civilization was very far away.

During our four day adventure, one float plane came in. Chubb Foster, a Maine guide, had wondered what we were doing. When he found that we knew how to camp and were skillful enough to keep our fires from destroying a wilderness, Foster showed us where he had cached an old canvas canoe. The trip was paradise, in spite of black flies and Bob's cooking. Then I had to write about it.

The article appeared in a national magazine aptly titled "Outdoors." It's long gone, but the publication was well read in its time. Unabashed and unconcerned, I told the story of Snake Pond and its great trout. With pictures–lots of pictures.

The magazine's check was fine, all $100 of it, and for more than a year there was no suspicion in my mind that an outdoor writer can be a Judas. Guilt seeped in when Chubb Foster wrote to say, sorrowfully, that "Snake Pond now looks like Richthofen's flying circus, and fish are scarce."

Everybody wanted *in*, and everybody got in. The grand trout were decimated and a "secret spot" was suddenly well known. I felt like a traitor.

Then, within another couple of years, one of the big lumber companies drove a tote road to Snake, and that–in the vernacular of the day–was "Katy bar the door!" There are no truly virgin waters on tote roads, so the lumberjacks lifted a few pounds of sorrow off my conscience.

That's why another small Maine pond became, in an article I wrote for another magazine, "The Lake North Of Lost Water." Top that for sneaky reporting!

I'm going back there soon again, and I won't tell you where it is—not unless you have me in a headlock. There's a tote road that ends a mile from the pond, and pretty soon those hungry pulp hunters will go all the way in.

Meanwhile, I plan to keep my tattered conscience partially intact.

Bug Time

Assuming that you are hero enough to bring this to friend wife's attention, there is no profit in declaring that pestiferous black flies, no-see-ums and mosquitoes are always the female of the species. Yet it's true: the males are noncombatants who lack a taste for human blood.

I don't know why I mentioned this in the first place, since I only want to emphasize the fact that northern trout and salmon fishing is at its peak when the bugs are biting.

Tub-thumpers in northern regions will tell you that sport fishing is magnificent from ice-out until the very end of the season. They are fine fellows, but they lie in their teeth. Thanks to the law of things as they are, it is quite impossible for any press agent to declare: "Come *now!* The bugs will eat you alive, but fishing is at an all-time peak."

This might be stark truth, but truth is a two-edged sword. Any public relations executive who admits the presence of a biting insect risks his job, if not his reputation as a huckster for whatever vacationland touted.

Personally, I like bugs. I like them because they signal the finest freshwater fishing of the entire year. When waters are warm enough to spawn mosquitoes, black flies and no-see-ums in astronomical numbers, trout get all fired up and grab anything that looks like a free meal.

It happens that the waters of our north country warm to this point between mid-May and mid-June. This is the jackpot season, especially if an angler desires to take his trout or salmon on the surface.

Now wilderness ponds and streams are delicately balanced. Snow water is long gone, but temperatures are still low enough to keep fish active in all stratas. More important, aquatic nymphs are rising to the sun, hatching by the billions.

Mayflies dance over black pools and flying ants descend in clouds. It is a time of opposites such as ice cold water and broiling sunlight, patches of dirty gray snow in the black growth, and smoke screens of midges in the alders.

Fishing will never be better, but neither will biting insects ever be so abundant. You must suffer to attain paradise, or so it seems to anglers who covet peak fishing in the north country.

First, there are the black flies. They are quite visible, and often appear harmless, but these insidious, soft-winged bugs must have teeth like saber-toothed tigers—for they can gouge out a tiny chunk of human flesh before you can move a hand in protest.

Initially, the wound bleeds, but is not particularly painful. Later, each black fly bite simulates the seven year itch. Poison ivy is balm by comparison.

No-see-ums lack bulk, but their fire power is based on numbers. Tiny as grains of animated pepper, the northern no-see-um or biting gnat (who, I have found, has a you-all counterpart in the Deep South called the sand fly) will drift through the finest netting. They are particularly fond of attacking the wrists, the neck, or the bare ankles of a human target.

Any well educated no-see-um can squirm like quicksilver under a shirt collar, a sleeve or a woolen sock to sink its miniscule fangs into *homo sapiens.* Worth noting is the fact that every no-see-um seems well educated in this respect.

Mosquitoes are more sporting, for they announce themselves with a high whine of engines. They're big enough to swat, although cagey enough to attack the right hand which is industriously working a reel handle and cannot be jarred during this delicate operation. If spinning gear is employed, they switch to the left hand.

There are certain defenses. One, obviously, is the head net affected by many anglers in the north country. This uncomfortable abortion will keep black flies at bay, but is no barrier against no-see-ums. Mosquitoes are catholic in their taste: they drill anywhere, but specialize in the hands and wrists of fishermen.

Insect repellents help, but should never be considered foolproof. Some of the bug-chasing concoctions will eat the varnish off a treasured split bamboo fly rod, but seem to have no affect upon the marauders. A majority of old timers in the back country rely on "fly dope" which smells like a catastrophe in a chemical factory, plus blue clouds of smoke from blackened pipes.

Smoke certainly discourages a given percentage of the bugs, but in order to be effective it must be so thick that the smoker chances nicotine poisoning. I prefer smoke, but I make no recommendations —especially now that my betters are cracking down on tobacco as a killer of humanity.

I can only tell you that the black fly, mosquito and no-see-um season is prime time to take a record trout or landlocked salmon in the wilderness lakes and streams of my north country. Therefore, bugs or no bugs, a lot of us will be there.

Once, not so many years ago, several of us terminated a great fishing excursion on Maine's West Branch of the Penobscot. The bugs were fierce, and the fishing was magnificent.

On the day we headed home, Arnold Laine, a great Massachusetts angler, was left on the scene of action. He had decided to stick it out for another week, protected by a new fly dope which he thought highly effective.

"This stuff," he declared, slapping at bare arms attacked by hordes of black flies, "discourages 80 per cent of the bugs!"

Then, still slapping, he muttered morosely and as an afterthought, "Sometimes that other 20 per cent gets mighty thick!"

Catch Report

At heart, every angler is a loner–but I like to have company on lake or stream. Paul Belton, my neighbor, had a day off and we talked about fishing together. Then I remembered an appointment with a visiting fireman at my Boston office.

Too late, it developed that our traveler had missed his plane and wouldn't be in. Suddenly I had a new minted day to spend, but Paul was long gone, off to some swamp where he hoped to creel a mess of brook trout.

Philosophically, I loaded a boat and decided to wire-line a local pond. It was too late in the morning for surface flies, and the June sun was tropical. Anyone who seeks trout on such a day ought to have his head examined.

The pond was mirror-smooth under a deep blue sky. There were no signs of life other than an occasional grackle planing through the jungle foliage of a summer shoreline. Even the water looked dusty with its skim of pollen.

Trolling can be great fun when fish oblige, but a blank day induces hypnosis. There's the engine's steady beat, the soft rise and fall of water under a moving keel–the pleasant nothingness that sometimes seems a waste of time.

At lunch hour I went ashore, driving the tin boat onto a little gravel bar beyond which an hourglass elm leaned over the water.

An ancient stone wall bordered a pasture here, and buttercups were blooming in its lee. I used a couple of sandwiches as an excuse to observe siesta.

Actually, no fisherman needs an alibi for relaxing. It's just that we hate to admit the delight of absorbing sunlight, of being completely quiet while all of Nature's beings go about their secret affairs. A well chosen nooning can be an experience in itself.

So I spent too much time watching a chipmunk who had no fear of man. Evidently other anglers had been here, for the striped atom refused a crust of bread, but he sat within a few inches of my outstretched hand, flirting his tail and visiting.

Then there were the ducks, a mallard hen and three of her half grown progeny. They came sculling up the shoreline and one of the ducklings unaccountably tapped the transom of my tin boat with its bill. They puddled through the shallows and ignored a red-tailed hawk balancing away up in the blue sky.

Granted, you see more when you're alone. Noise and movement alarms some of the wild creatures. If I'd had a garrulous companion the woodchuck might not have ventured into a nearby edge to crop clover and, later, to climb into the low crotch of a wild cherry tree. Why'd he do that? I don't know. Maybe just to get a better view of the wide world.

I'm a hunter—in season—and yet I could not have blasted that 'chuck out of his eyrie. There was no garden within sight and he destroyed nothing but a few leaves of clover. I'd learned that wood-chucks, if they so desire, can climb trees. That was important. Fishing was lousy, so I went home.

Paul arrived while I was weeding a back yard tomato patch in the last glow of sunset. He'd been similarly afflicted. The swamp trout were still there, if ever they had been. He'd caught two dace on a dry fly.

"Terrible day," he muttered, and then began to tell me about surprising a deer, seeing a beaver and watching two kingbirds attack a crow.

The deer was a doe in red summer pelage, belly-deep in the stream when Paul's canoe came snaking around an alder-screened bend. She'd raised her head and looked at him for a long moment. What fodder do they find in a cold trout stream? Or was she simply bathing, escaping the flies?

Gracefully, not at all alarmed, the doe had turned and melted into the bright green shrubbery of June. Paul caught a flickering impression of that impossibly white tail as she went through the alders and up a birch slope.

On this stream beavers had been working, their shiny yellow cuttings everywhere in evidence. Once the burgeoning civilization of our north country had exterminated these big rodents, but now they are re-established to a point of occasional concern.

Belton's canoe had rounded another bend, into a backwater, when he saw something that looked like a swimming spaniel or an outsized muskrat. But only for a moment. Then the beaver's flat, paddle-like tail slapped the water with a report like a pistol shot. It dove and was gone.

Later, nooning as I had done, he watched a crow beating across the sky while two kingbirds harried it unmercifully. For all the world that crow looked like a lumbering bomber attacked by two fighter planes. Finally the kingbirds veered off, probably satisfied that their nesting site had been protected.

Terrible day? Granted, neither of us had succeeded in catching a limit of fish. We can blame that on the weather, carefully camouflaging our own lack of skill. Maybe we'll forget the day itself, because there were no trophies to boast about.

But I think in the end of it—without fanfare but infinitely more important—we'll remember such slices of life in the boondocks as a duckling testing a tin boat by rapping it with its bill, a sated, sun-loving woodchuck climbing into a cherry tree, a trusting chipmunk, a beaver's tail-slapping departure, and two kingbirds performing faultless pursuit curves around a harried crow.

I'd like to have seen Paul's deer—surprised, but hardly alarmed, the clean, cold water dripping from her snout. All of it happened in a whispering woodland where a fisherman can be part of the landscape.

I won't try to explain the feeling, nor will any sportsman. You either know, or it isn't worth discussion. The wonder and the innocence of Nature might sound square in a world too practical to express simple delight.

Elegy For a Ruffed Grouse

They hammered at the door, two neighborhood youngsters with the usual burden–a wild creature in trouble.

This time it was a female ruffed grouse, a handsome little biddy with four tail feathers missing and one leg that had been immobilized. The boys only knew that it was "caught in a bush and couldn't fly."

I'm always mournful when country lads think that an old hunter and naturalist can perform miracles. Although the bird was bright-eyed and, true to its kind, unafraid–I knew that it was doomed. Almost certainly this delicate chicken of the woodlands had collided with a motor vehicle.

The grouse lived overnight, resting in a wire-meshed cage that I reserve for wild transients until such time as they can be picked up by a representative of the state's Department of Natural Resources, and then it expired quietly. In due time I'll perform an autopsy and seek to discover the cause and extent of its injuries, but my findings will be unimportant.

Nor is there any panacea. Our mechanized society is a greater threat to wildlife than all of the world's hunters and natural predators. The automobile, the lethal spray of DDT, the deadly trace of mercury and the advance of a cement and steel civilization make the inroads of predators and gunners a minor affliction.

The grouse I bury in June might have reared a whole phalanx of sturdy fliers for November gunners. Now it's dead and–somewhere in nearby woodlands–half-grown chicks are lost and probably destined to perish. Nature is a grim taskmaster.

Well-meaning folk sometimes rail against hunters who take a small, fair share of game during a short open shooting period. Too few seem concerned about the off-season slaughter of wildlife, perhaps because this is a by-product of a thing we call progress.

I'm not about to clamor for curbs on highway travel or bans on new housing developments and necessary agricultural sprays, but I can't accept a double standard in logic. Our civilization is killing our wilderness and the death rate is catastrophic.

Moreover, we in America have no real idea of the actual kill. We see cottontail rabbits, gray squirrels, pheasants, grouse and assorted lesser creatures ground into the roadbeds or thrown into the gutters. Hundreds of deer share the same fate every year, in every suburban township of this nation.

Sudden death is shocking, even when a bird or animal is the victim. Poison sprays and mercury compounds are more insidious, for they murder slowly and secretly. *Silent Spring?*

Maybe there's macabre poetic justice here, for the toxic substances that kill bugs and birds are accumulating in the tissues of mankind. Every human being on this earth carries the space-age poisons in his body. Some of these malignant deposits never recede, break down, or are expelled: they only continue to build up. Perhaps we are engaged in universal suicide.

Progress is synonymous with development. Granted, America boasts vast undeveloped acreage. When you fly over this tremendous land of ours, the woodland still dominates. Unfortunately, or perhaps fortunately if you're an empire builder, the cement and steel lava flow expands with each passing year. Wild ducks retreat when marshes are filled. Bluebirds become a legend as farmlands disappear. Deer drift back to the outskirts.

While do-gooders argue about game hogs who take more than their share of trout, great industrial complexes gobble up complete trout streams and reduce them to trickling seeps of oily pollution. There are laws against the plucking of certain wildflowers, but none to curb the developer who bulldozes an entire hillside, burns its trees and buries its life-giving streams.

Those who fight the trend find themselves an unpopular minority. Progress is a strange word, and it doesn't always mean a step forward for the multitudes. Too often progress means power for the few at the expense of natural resources which enrich the many. Hunters are pikers in the rape of the wild things.

So, I come full circle! As a gunner, I delight in the clean kill of a ruffed grouse towering over white birches in November. Make the most of it if you charge me with hypocrisy when I mourn a hen partridge struck down by an automobile in June.

Perhaps she challenged the speeding car, instinctively protecting her clutch of immatures. Someone failed to apply the brakes in time, or simply didn't care, and so I have a bird to bury—plus a nagging suspicion that a half-dozen young grouse will be lost.

All of us, whether hunters, Nature lovers, or simply citizens who delight in a balanced wilderness, will lose. We fight for the same things and we are thwarted by a civilization which seems to regard all of the wild creatures as expendable.

Sea Change

If inland fishing is tranquility, then salt water angling has to be fury. That's generalization, and I'll tell you how it works.

Driving east, from central Massachusetts to Cape Cod, I applied certain blue water words to the gale—which was fresh enough to jolt my scurrying motor car. Still, it was a Friday afternoon with a big weekend dead ahead.

It takes about three hours, give or take minutes depending on traffic, to make this run. Then, if you're a beach buggy angler, another hour may be consumed in loading up, fueling the Jeep and bouncing out to a chosen location on Provincetown's fishing grounds. By the time I arrived on target the sun was almost gone.

There was the usual optical illusion. Sometimes you'd swear that the sea resists entry, and so the sun seems to spread, to widen its base and bulge into a flaming mushroom cap as it plunges over the western horizon.

One delightful product of salt water angling is a sense of continual change. On this evening I took a few moments to absorb the fact that our mid-day wind had subsided. At dusk, as the first stars glittered overhead, there wasn't a whisper.

As usual, I'd planned to fish a night tide—with visions of creaming surf and big stripers walloping small bait. If the day's gale had been discouraging, this flat calm was quite as defeating. A surfman wants *some* suds, for marine fish come alive in churning waters.

But you don't argue with the elements, so I hiked a sand beach where the ground swell arrived with a liquid rustle instead of a crash. Small bait flickered on the mirror-like surface, but my plugs were unmolested.

There is something almost weird about an absolutely still night on the sea-rim. Sound is amplified, where normally it would be swallowed up in the boom of breakers and the sibilant rush of clicking sand particles as the waves rush back.

The hooded surfmen, those enthusiasts who are never seen by daylight, moved like sleep-walkers. The long, expiring sigh of their reels was followed by the plops of lures dropping in. Muted conversation was punctuated by the occasional squawk of a dozing gull.

Race Point's foghorn was silent, but the ubiquitous light swung in its predetermined arc. Each time that swath of white beamed across the famous rip it touched the fluttering wings of petrels. Mother Carey's chickens are small sea birds of the open ocean, remarkable because they appear to walk on the water and feed by night as well as by day.

At length spiny dogfish appeared, cruising almost alongshore, feeding on the small bait which flocked in the shallows. A dogfish endangers no human being, but the creature boasts a skin rough enough to cut any line with which it comes in contact. Surf casters usually quit when dogs move in.

So I retired to a sleeping bag, and the following day was quite as hot and still. In mid-afternoon I cased surf rods and sped back to central Massachusetts, hoping to find rainbow trout walloping flies in this blessed June stillness.

That didn't work, either. Sunday found a fresh southwest gale whipping across Belchertown's Swift River. Sunlight was achingly brilliant and the trout had declared a moritorium.

Just to rub salt in accustomed wounds, I later heard that Provincetown's surfmen enjoyed great striped bass fishing that morning. So the elements can deflate egos and make predictions look like any weather man's forecast. One of these days I'll hit it right.

Dr. Doolittle

You will understand, of course, that there exists between men and boys a wide gap that cannot be bridged without the aid of absolute genius or plain, dumb luck. Common sense, logic and the will to cooperate meet with cool disdain, and that's because the clock of life can't be turned back.

I'm middle-aged, and yet I seem to have achieved some rapport with neighborhood youngsters. At least they wreak no havoc upon my goods, and they come to me with important problems—such as the care of pet turtles and the possibility of taming a young wood-chuck captured in some stone-walled corner.

Granted, neighborhood kids may view me as a strange old duffer who's forever flying off to some remote sea or wilderness, but when I return from the outermost rim of the world they know that I'll be engaged in something quite sane and practical—like raising caterpillars.

What's wrong with raising caterpillars? The kids come and peer at these crawly wonders. Unlike too many adults, they can believe that a green worm may turn into a magnificent silk moth. Moreover, I can show them each stage in the long journey—egg, larvae, cocoon and triumphant winged insect. They learn something of value, and they're primed to learn because their minds are still flexible enough

79

to choose something other than a myth which is founded on ignorance or fear.

I think it important for youngsters to know that a garter snake is beneficial, that toads are good friends because they devour garden insects, that skunks won't bother you unless you bother them. Youngsters are apt students, especially when the course is all outdoors.

There's nothing like a practical demonstration to convince kids, and I must admit that the old black art of magic helps.

In July, our back yard is a close-cropped expanse of green grass and clover. Cottontail rabbits feed there, and I talk to them. If the neighbors feel that I'm a harmless nut, the children are suitably impressed. In time, they'll figure it out—and then they'll be more intelligent citizens.

No legerdemain is involved, of course. All wild creatures are mesmerized by cadenced sound. If you walk quietly toward a rabbit on your lawn, he'll bound away before you are within fifty feet of his position. In this case you're a threatening presence, something to fear and to avoid.

But, if you speak softly as you approach, the rabbit will be lulled and strangely immobilized by the human voice. Talk to a wild cottontail and, in no time at all, you will be able to approach within a dozen steps. Youngsters get saucer-eyed at a demonstration, and some adults begin to wonder—although, lacking the empirical logic of youth, they'll seek avenues of escape.

Experienced hunters know that sound can be put to use. Those of us who love gun sport kill nothing in July, other than the woodchuck systematically destroying a garden, yet we recall that a cadenced approach flushes ruffed grouse close to the gun in November, and that steady sound rarely spooks a whitetailed deer in December.

I remember an afternoon in the Maine woods, above Lake Sebago, when Bob Williams and I, shuffling along and discussing a buck that had been reduced to possession the day before, practically bumped into a pair of does that had been standing quietly, obviously mesmerized by the steady sound of human voices.

Perhaps it is unfair for a hunter to employ such tactics, as the best of them do in those months which are set aside for harvest. Fortunately for game birds and mammals, very few gunners invoke the old magic.

If there's any secret, it lies in cadence and familiarity. Annually I talk to robins and catbirds and wrens. If you're cautious about it, and persistent, you'll soon be able to approach these birds on their nests without shocking them into frenzied flight. Gradually they come to recognize a voice and to fear no evil from the recognized human visitor. Anyone can do this.

Curiously, it works with a wide variety of wild creatures—and tame ones as well. Snatching at a domestic dog may well result in nipped fingers, but friendships are launched when you speak quietly, offer a quiet hand to be sniffed and appraised. Magicians who understand the process soon have chickadees and chipmunks eating out of their hands. Resist quick movement and the skulking approach. Speak softly and rely on cadenced sound. If you do these things you enter the world of the wild and the timorous.

Directly across the street from my home lives a collie dog named Beauty. She's a lovely animal, much given to smiling—a thing achieved by too few dogs. Occasionally I have a scrap of steak or some other leftover which is admirably suited to the attention of a healthy collie. I don't call her by name: instead, I step out on the back porch and—bark.

Neighbors may consider this slightly unusual, but Beauty is tuned in: she's on her way before the third yelp has sounded. We are communicating.

The fact that this exchange had strengthened my nebulous rapport with youngsters was brought home when a next-door neighbor, who happens to be a burly state police officer, ventured a question.

"The kids tell me you speak dog language," he grinned. "Who you trying to fool?"

So I called up Beauty with two yelps, and then—just to be a show-off—I bawled at his son Danny's black angus cow. The cow lifted her head and made it appear that the "word" went home.

I hadn't conditioned her, as I had the dog, and I don't think she knows me, but I rest my case.

Gone Frogging

You'd be surprised to hear how expeditions are planned. For example, I blueprinted a frogging trip while a plastic eel was bouncing along behind a twin-screw cruiser some twenty-five miles south of Rhode Island.

One white marlin had been brought to boat and another had finned out, looked at our baits and disappeared into cobalt depths. It was hot and sunny out there, the sea a twinkling vastness in every direction. Big game fishing means hours of hypnotic, rocking boredom interspersed with short bursts of furious action.

Therefore blue water anglers find lots of time to discuss the important things in life, like the savor of frogs' legs browned in sizzling butter. Someone noted that Louisiana had been "over-frogged" and that nobody seemed to harvest these delicacies in our northern states. I had; and immediately decided to do so again.

Frogging is an ancient and honorable art. In the Deep South commercial operators use shallow, flat-bottomed boats, together with three-tined spears and miners' headlights. These specialists usually work at night and they supply high priced entrees for gourmets.

Yankee froggers rarely, if ever, toil for the market. In our north country a harvest is deemed satisfactory if it provides one memorable meal.

First, of course, you have to catch a frog. Indeed, considering the size of northern bullfrogs, a dozen of them might be necessary to provide a main course. There are several methods, not excluding the small boy's quick hand.

Frogs can be caught on rod and line. A Red Ibis fly has been touted as most effective, but red flannel on an ordinary single hook will do the job. A hungry bullfrog must be nearsighted, for anything that flies is considered fair game. (My brother once coaxed successive "strikes" at a fluttering white daisy bloom suspended from the tip of a fly rod!)

Therefore, if you are so inclined, a fly or a tiny patch of red cloth on a hook is dangled just in front of a crouching prize. If the thing whisks close enough, he'll capture it with a long and sticky tongue. Some aggressive bullfrogs will chase the offering for yards.

This technique is deadly—and I want no part of it. Bullfrogs may be cold blooded, as the bookmen say, and practically incapable of feeling pain, but I have seen too many of them fighting a line. If I must kill to harvest a gourmet dinner, let that killing be swift. No hooks or sharp spears for me: I prefer a hollow-nosed .22 caliber bullet.

That's why, on the day following an offshore trip in which I had landed and released a handsome white marlin, I waded the shore of a marginal pond. Deer flies buzzed about my head. Grackles protested. The sun was hot and there was no wind. I heard the occasional chunking notes of frogs in the lily pads and shoreside weeds. Wading, feeling the soft mud squeeze into my sneakers, I was happier than a man should be. It was like a return to youth, only the frogs wouldn't cooperate. My light rifle's bore remained clean and bright.

The frogs were there, but smaller than I'd imagined. Little reticulated leopard frogs leaped out of my path. Tiny jug-a-rums sat on lily pads and regarded me with their bulging, jewel-like eyes. There seemed nothing of a size to harvest.

So I circumnavigated the pond, startled a great blue heron fishing for shiners and watched a kit muskrat sitting on a hummock and scrubbing his face. Wash-up? Or were his whiskers itchy? Darned if I know.

At any rate it was pleasant in there, what with a few blueberries to nibble and with cool water halfway up my legs to defeat the humidity of July. I almost forgot the cradled gun: dreams of a frogs' leg dinner had evaporated.

But then I remembered a spring, a carefully scooped-out hole in an adjacent hillside where some farmer had encouraged a trickle of water. No spring is without a giant bullfrog–and a tin cup left by a thirsty samaritan.

The alders were higher than I recalled them, but the great oak was just where it has been since George Washington slept in diverse northern inns. I peered over a shielding hedge of fern: the water was there like a dark mirror–and a huge frog sat on a mossy rock.

He was the kind of frog I'd anticipated–big enough to provide part of that long anticipated gourmet dinner. Stealthily, I raised the rifle and centered its knife-blade front sight on his wide, squat head.

Immobile, he still moved. His sides breathed evenly. The pouch under his chin pulsed slowly, rythmically. He was wet and dry at the same time–a comfortable damp, satiny green creature at rest. I'd never seen a larger bullfrog in the North.

Unfortunately, large as he was, I realized that one frog would never make a meal. No sentiment, mind you, just logic. So I lowered the rifle, unconsciously surrendering. Frogs' legs are fine, but I'd have to settle for something else.

Maybe that's the story of my life, but I'm going frogging again this week. A colleague has told me of a swamp where the jug-a-rums are three to a hummock and big enough to scare a timber wolf. I don't believe a word of it, yet I've cancelled a giant tuna junket. The tuna will be around for a month or so, and I want to nail a mess of frogs' legs while they're still available.

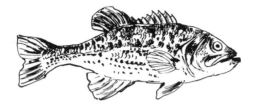

Bronzeback in the Night

Now it is deep summer and jungle foliage crowds a livid sunset horizon. Lightning bugs punctuate the dusk and insects shrill. I have tasted trout in May and the first fury of striped bass in June. Now the scent of sweet flag hangs heavy on the air–and I want a black bass.

Not any ordinary bass, but a huge bronzeback in the night. I want him to be secretive, prowling the tropical shoreline of a northern pond in July–a pugnacious warrior and a wary one. I want him to play hard to get, until he falls for a plug I'll cast and retrieve so artfully that he can't resist socking it!

Once, in central New England, the black bass fishing season began on July 1. Nowadays the species is legal much earlier, but we used to make our first casts at midnight, just as June melted into July. This is no longer necessary, but moonlighters rarely forget their beginnings.

A bass in the dark hours is a strange and wonderful fish. He is something out of fairy tales, a villain, an ogre. There is delicious strangeness in this angling, a beauty never captured in harsh daylight. The scents and the sights and the sounds are subtly changed.

Black bass are nocturnal fish during the deep summer months in our northland. They feed by day, but only sporadically, darting out from their cover of lily pads and pickerel weed to engulf hapless

85

minnows or frogs. By night these aggressive gladiators roam the shallows, gobbling everything from smaller fish to swimming mice and huge summer night moths.

To me, the scent of citronella is an essence of black bass. This aromatic oil has always been a basic mosquito repellent, and I suspect it is on a par with the new spray mixtures. At any rate the combination of citronella, sweet flag and the pleasant perfume of clean inland waters is a medley of delight.

There is so much more to black bass fishing than a midnight safari replete with nostalgic aromas. There is the black and silver surface of a lake, darkly mirroring trees and sky. There is the stertorous croaking of frogs and the piercing love song of a whippoorwill. There is always a muskrat, vee-lining his way across the mirror, all unconcerned about the human animal standing so quietly on the shore.

And then there is the bass. He, or she—for I am not concerned about the sex of bass—is a spirit of the night. This compact, volatile fish is vibrantly alive during the hushed, dark hours of deep summer.

You cast to a well remembered snag, not seeing it, but recalling its location. You cast along the shore, close to a dock which serves pleasure boatmen in garish daylight hours—and the lure comes wriggling back etched by thin starlight. Here is another slice of that tranquility Izaak Walton wrote about—a delicious spice of mystery and, when a fish strikes, high adventure.

A black bass must have eyes like an owl, for it can nail a lure on the darkest of nights. Savagely and with astonishing accuracy this fish storms to the attack. He strikes a bait solidly, thrashing until spray gleams white against the dark ripples, and then races into the depths to wage a bulldog war of resistance.

Beaten at last, either kept as a trophy or released to fight again, the northern bronzeback remains a thing of the wild. In a flashlight's gleam his eyes glow like opals and he works his gills spasmodically. In spite of mosquitoes and the tendency to wade over one's boot tops, there is much to be said for black bass fishing on a summer night.

The Magic Island

So far as I am concerned, the island of Cuttyhunk huddles in a thick fog and is forever whipped by gale force winds. It is always night-time there, and it is bitterly cold. The sea is uncomfortably choppy—and striped bass fishing verges on the spectacular.

Inland, the thermometer bubbled at 82 degrees as a blaze-orange sun mushroomed and melted into the western horizon. We met at Padenarum, near New Bedford, where the sea breeze was cool after a blistering day. Kib Bramhall had driven in from Newton, Massachusetts, and Stuart Hunter wryly admitted that he'd been nailed for speeding on the Connecticut Turnpike, en route from Philadelphia.

Capt. Frank Sabatowski and his *June Bug II,* a fine little Cuttyhunk-MacKenzie bass boat, were waiting at the slip. We lugged our duffel aboard—rods and tackle boxes, foul weather gear and cameras. This time the weather seemed to be cooperating.

But never count on fine weather off those strange atolls which make up the Elizabeth Island chain on the shoulder of Cape Cod. There is an elemental mixer here, and its prime ingredient is fury. Men subject to mal de mer should steer clear of the Elizabeths.

Before we cast off the sun had plunged into oblivion and stars were twinkling overhead. There was no sea making, and the sound was quiet—it stretched ahead of us, wrinkled like blue velvet. Over the throaty roar of our engine we caught the strains of a dance band radioed from a cruising yacht.

Skirting that far island of Cuttyhunk, on whose precipitous slopes the dwelling houses of seafaring men send splintered rays of incandescent light over the deep-breathing Atlantic, we steered a course for Devil's Bridge, just off Martha's Vineyard. There, according to Sabatowski, the tide would be "right" shortly before midnight.

And it was, and we caught four big stripers. These hulking brutes, each weighing between 40 and 45 pounds, belted swimming plugs trolled deep in the swift rips. Although a strong and confused cross-chop had developed, we laid it to the clashing currents and we were too busy to think about weather.

There were other boats in the area, drifting in and out of the slot, dropping back to gaff great bass and then churning ahead to maintain their chosen positions. Above us, and to the left, Gay Head's light periodically swept the seas. Kib was first to notice the fog.

It drifted in from eastward, partially obscuring the light. Imperceptibly, our warm night cooled, and then it was downright chilly. The wind freshened, a curious thing in fog. Suddenly we were isolated in an opaque veil of misty, milky cloud—and the seas were rising.

Sabatowski fired up and we headed back across the sound toward Cuttyhunk. Halfway there, with bitter salt spume dashing over the bow and our illuminated depth-finder oscillating madly, the skipper fractured my cool.

"Did you ever have the feeling that your compass wasn't working?"

But Sabby knew what he was doing and the compass was in good repair. In these rock-studded waters one had best take no chances. Peering at the dimly illuminated instruments he said, finally: "We're pretty close to Quick's Hole, so we'll anchor and wait for dawn."

That was one of the longest waits I have ever experienced, and I am an old campaigner. We wrapped ourselves in all available woolens and oilskins and we huddled in the cuddy. There was wind, and it was bitterly cold. The chill mist embraced us and it seemed that dawn would never come.

But, finally, the east paled. Our fog bank was still there, glowing like a fire opal. The wind whistled and waves spat icy spray over the gunwales. Midsummer in Massachusetts? You'd never believe it!

Wild currents were churning through Quick's Hole and we maneuvered for position. The rigs went over, now bucktail-dressed lures on short wire lines. Suddenly, with strengthening light, sea birds came to scream and wheel over the sudsy ground swells.

With them, stripers! Legions of bass were there in the rips and they hit our lures so regularly that we soon forgot the night and the cold. Sweat succeeded chill and we tonged those wonderful fish in the pearlescent dawn.

Then, quite suddenly, it was all over. The mist had burned off and the sea was blue. The birds were gone and the wind had subsided to a murmur. The cold magic of Cuttyhunk was only a memory.

So we went back to the docks at Padenarum and we blinked drowsily in hot sunlight. Once again it was midsummer, with the temperature winding up for a scorcher.

I still think that Cuttyhunk is an island bathed in mist and swept by high winds, that it is always nighttime there, and always bitterly cold. In fact, I hate the place.

But I'll be back, if only because those rough seas and chill winds guarantee some of the best striped bass fishing in this blue-eyed world.

Tranquility Regained

That morning I had jetted in from Costa Rica—hot, tired, sunburned and nursing memories of great sea sport on the wild, Pacific side of that delightful country in Central America. Any sane man would have slept, but it was mid-July in my north country. Moreover, the day was fresh and sparkling with dew. I went fishing.

There is much to be said for big game and far-away places, for sophisticated tackle and high adventure on salt water, but reserve a full measure of appreciation for the tiny battlers of a shallow northern pond, for basic equipment and the quiet approach which insures tranquility.

On this clean, brilliant morning my pond was placid, mirror-like, adorned with pickerel weed that thrust arrowheaded spikes above the surface. Pond lilies wafted a thin perfume into the humid air. Nobody was in attendance, unless I cite three black ducks that, characteristically, spattered off to land somewhere along the far eastern shore.

The gravel road was bordered with white daisies and there was a little turn-around where generations of small boat skippers had launched. When I shoved my canoe into the water a bullfrog protested irritably and belly-flopped off his vantage point on a hummock. Almost immediately he surfaced to regard me with bulging, jeweled eyes.

Power boats are fine, but too many of us have forgotten the subtle thrills of paddling a canoe. There is satisfaction in it, together with a wonderful feeling of buoyancy. The craft is alive, responsive to each twist of an ash blade. On a silent pond, the swish and chuckle of water makes music to compliment birdsong.

Best of all, from a canoe drifting on a clear, clean pond, one can almost believe in levitation. A glimpse over the gunwale discloses a veritable troll's garden with patches of white sand and chocolate mud a fathom deep; water weeds streaming like lace in a lazy current, and minnows cruising in nervous schools.

Nothing in the wilderness minds a canoe. The great blue heron stalks his prey unafraid. Kingfishers rattle overhead and muskrats draw their fine vee-lines across the surface. Perhaps you may be fortunate enough to see a deer on a point of land, or a mother otter teaching her sprouts how to catch suckers.

Dispensing with an outboard motor, you melt into the landscape and hear the voices of the wild creatures—a steady background melody of frogs chunking and toads trilling. The purple grackles are always very busy, sounding their harsh, metallic "chek, chek," and no morning would be complete without the hoarse, immeasurably wild challenge of a cock pheasant from a nearby hill.

Every small pond offers a legion of delights. You can drift in the shallows, casting for bluegills: they hit miniature flies with the greatest of abandon. Or, if you are so inclined, anchor in ten or twelve feet of water and catch yellow perch or horned pout on plebian angleworms. This is an admirable way to spend a leisurely morning.

If bigger game beckons, there are always pickerel in the shade of the weed beds. Sometimes you can spot them lying like slim torpedoes, hardly moving a fin to maintain balance and position. Skittering is most effective on pickerel at this time of year, and the best bait is a strip cut from the belly of a small yellow perch. Angleworms or nightcrawlers will do in a pinch, but they are neither physically nor psychologically right. In our north country a perch belly's the trick for skittering.

Of course the fish are just part of it, and perhaps of minor importance. They offer an excuse to get out there, away from telephones and traffic and outboard motors, a chance to do things that are quite natural.

Like shedding shoes and shirts. It would be nice to shed more, but people would talk so! Like racking the rods to inspect a particularly fine growth of pond lilies–and perhaps to collect a few long-stemmed beauties which, in a shallow bowl, will open each morning to exude a delightful fragrance.

There is much to be said for landing on a floating island to prospect high bush blueberries. Two to one they'll still be green, but there'll be enough of the ripe fruit to assuage a sudden hunger. Moreover, you may find the nest of a vireo and surprise a painted turtle far from protecting water. There will be pitcher plants, devouring insects; wild bees humming in the buttonbrush, and–over all–a sweet-and-rotten scent of high summer as vegetation cycles from green sprout to full foliage and, finally, to decay.

All of it is reassuring; even where suburbia crowds down to the shores, our wilderness remains within reach. There is clean water and solitude, birds and small mammals and insects multitudinous. Fish are biting, although they are not the monsters of tropical seas, and one can enjoy royal sport without calling upon the marvels of science.

I came back to the landing: it was a shelving gravel bank with a huge slab of granite at its head and garnished with white daisies. Harvest? A half-dozen bluegills, large enough to fillet and broil; two big yellow perch, wonderful table fare; a hat full of blueberries and a slithery wealth of waterlilies. They were the huge white ones that smell like a preacher's description of heaven.

Plus more sunburn and honest sweat. Plus lower blood pressure induced by tranquility and communion with a quiet, marginal pond. No thundering motors. No great game fish in exotic waters. Just cool mud between the toes and a grand sense of fulfilment. The bullfrog belly-flopped again, and again rose to question me with his gold-flecked eyes.

Perhaps I am a local yokel, but I think it very hard to top our northland in July.

Summer Interlude

Last week I was chasing striped bass in a high wind off Cape Cod, and three days hence I'll be flying down to Norfolk, Virginia for a crack at white marlin. Right now I'm going to do something quite as important. Nothing.

Pull up a lawn chair and join the club.

I'm going to sit here in my back yard, sans shirt, and let the sun tan my carcass. Ever notice that as you put on middle-aged weight you get a fat man's tan? There are white creases where you overlap! Dammit, I'm not fat—but the white strips call me a liar.

Much can be said for gainful labor, yet I promote the occasional do-nothing hour. Like a kid with a whole summer vacation to waste, it's fine to look at cloud formations, at green grass and trees. Just look. You'll find there's a lot to see. Surprising how much a guy can learn, just sitting in his own back yard.

Like all egotistical humans I entertain the fantastic notion that this little strip of lawn and shrubbery, bordered by tall trees, belongs to me and mine. There, after all, are my tomato plants and flowers. Away down where the trees begin and the shadows are blue, there is the grave of a beloved dog, marked by a rough field-stone and a clump of irises. My stamping grounds? Nonsense!

This land really belongs to a whole host of creatures who accept me as a necessary evil. There are the tree swallows, prescribing graceful aerobatics as they capture flying insects. They've raised a family here and, very shortly, the whole tribe will be migrating to wherever tree swallows go as the year spins out.

We have rabbits. They're pests, but I haven't the heart to shoot them, so I talk to the little cusses. They've eaten every sunflower I planted in May and they seek out the clover that our lawn mower has missed. The cottontails rarely acknowledge my presence. They know that I'm a harmless old duffer, and some of them are so mesmerized by the human voice that I can walk right up to them, talking all the time—muttering nonsense that might put me in an institution with rubber walls were it recorded.

I'm an inveterate reader, but this is no time for books. Binoculars are better. The magic of the lens and the mirror brings me and my wild neighbors eyeball to eyeball. Lord knows why I can enjoy successive performances of birds in a bird-bath. They throw water hell west and crooked. Robins, catbirds and starlings are great bathers. Bluejays drink a lot, but they don't wade right in.

Some romantic soul advised me that orioles can be vectored in by a half-orange hung in a tree. I tried it, and it doesn't work. My orioles flash around the premises, but they aren't intrigued by oranges. Matter of fact, I don't know why I call them "my orioles," since they belong to the whole wide world.

So do the butterflies that waltz across the lawn. There are yellow swallowtails and a host of fritilaries. Bright red *Monarchs* sample the flowers—and I find myself wondering if they'll migrate to Florida or California. They can, you know.

The larvae of the *Monarch* is a tiger-striped green caterpillar that feeds on milkweed. For some reason it is sensitive to sound, so you can cause it to jink like a startled snipe by coughing or shouting. Are you willing to raise eyebrows by shouting at a caterpillar?

I am, but I won't. I simply plan to sit here and look at a whole back yard world of living things. Certainly a bumblebee or two will come to buzz me, but they won't sting because bumblebees are gentlemen. They observe the old rule—don't lean on me and I won't lean on you.

We all check the stock market reports and we worry about our nation's economy. The birds and the insects and the beasties couldn't care less, and maybe they have the right idea.

I think it's a pretty good dodge to spend some time sprawled out in a lawn chair, divorced from commerce and far from a telephone. Now and then there is virtue in doing precisely nothing.

Toads Make Warts!

Generally I agree with the caustic character, probably W. C. Fields, who said: "Take a boy fishing, and throw the little rascal overboard!"

But every now and then I meet a youngster who is completely enthralled by the great outdoors, and then I hearken back to myself, fifty years ago. Kids never change.

This red-haired, ten year old brat had to share a seat with me on a jet flying from Chicago to Boston. He squirmed for a while and began to look pleased when I offered him the window seat. At 36,000 feet the ground looked like nothing more than a topo map, yet boys have a compulsion to see for themselves.

Gradually he began to talk and, curiously, we had much in common. For one thing, he liked to "fly" darning needles. I haven't done that since Methuselah was a boy.

This lad convinced me that times change, but youth is eternal. He spends his summers on a farm in Wellesley and he has absorbed all of the wonderful fantasies which make life a glorious adventure. We yammered away like two old topers—me with my airline-allotted two belts of Scotch on the rocks, and he with a soft drink.

It seems that a toad can give you warts, that a snake's forked tongue is his "stinger," that grasshoppers exude molasses, and that a horsehair, left in a watering trough, will shortly turn into a snake.

This was a boy who believed in spitting on his bait for luck. He probably worried about a black cat crossing his path, and he wouldn't walk under ladders. I'm sure he hacks paths through the woods and builds tree houses. Give him another few years and he'll be kissing pretty girls every time a firefly blinks in the humid August nighttime.

Because I once harbored similar illusions, it was only charitable to be surprised about the toad's elixir of warts, the garter snake's flickering "stinger," and the fact that a horsehair can spring into life. These are gems in the folklore of America. Generations of kids have become saucer-eyed in the telling and retelling of such fairy tales. Grimm's old world heroes and heroines were never more real.

And yet I wondered if this lad believed his own flights of fancy. Perhaps he was putting me on, secretly chuckling. Toads afflict no human beings with warts. The forked tongue of a snake is a sensory organ, not a stinger, and horsehairs remain horsehairs, in or out of water.

The ancient idea that a grasshopper produces molasses or tobacco juice is intriguing. A majority of today's children wouldn't recognize molasses if they saw or tasted it, yet a captured grasshopper does drool a dark, amber liquid which, in my youth, was supposed to be either molasses or tobacco juice.

It doesn't taste like either. Years ago I made the test and added to a growing fund of disillusionment.

Well then, according to all country boys, a snake doesn't die until sunset, no matter how hacked and tormented. Moreover, if you kill a snake its mate will come looking for you. Some snakes milk cows and others form themselves into hoops, the better to roll down hill. Any snake can charm a bird.

Woodchucks always emerge to look for their shadows on the second day of February, and bats are blind. Whippoorwills suckle goats. It'll rain if you step on a bug, and it's fierce bad luck to kill a cricket.

Perhaps such fairy tales are necessary: they add spice to the humdrum journal of existence. Boys and girls need a share of romantic fiction, and maybe they always regard the tall tale as just that. Even so, the magic remains.

My red-haired friend really stopped me with the dragonfly bit. After explaining that a darning needle can sew your mouth shut, another old superstition which is dear to the hearts of children, he declared that he liked to "fly" them on a string.

Shades of hide and seek! No red-blooded American boy of the Lindbergh era failed to fly darning needles. Now, jetting through a high, blue sky, this youngster told me just how it is done. I listened and nodded my head at appropriate intervals. It would have been criminal to tell him that boys have been doing this for years—worse to admit that I, a gray-haired ancient, had once embraced the sport.

Youthful barbarians of my day—and this—catch big dragonflies in nets. It isn't easy, because the insects are fast and erratic. Having succeeded in this initial quest, one must handle the prisoner with care, for his gauzy wings are fragile and his body a paper-thin shell of chitin and soft tissue.

Once reduced to possession, as the game biologists like to say, a fine thread is knotted about the darning needle's body, just back of the thorax and wings. You can "fly" one for hours, and then let the creature go back to hawking after mosquitoes.

I'd like to try it again, but I don't think I will. It's all very well to raise caterpillars and talk to rabbits, but any grown man flying a darning needle at the end of a thread might well be placed under surveillance.

Serves us right, too, for getting old and stuffy.

Lost Art

Old gaffers assume that their way is best–and usually they are wrong, since youth always advances. Today's trapshooters are more accurate than their fathers, and the modern fly-caster is dropping feather lures far beyond the marks scored by former greats.

I offer this observation, frankly, as a sop to youngsters–before I tell them that they have lost one of the greatest pickerel fishing techniques in this delightful world.

Back a few years, in fact so far back that I barely saw the end of it, and I am an ancient fellow, skittering was the deadliest of all techniques. It is still so deadly that it ought to be outlawed, but I am going to tell you how and why it works.

Prior to bait casting and spin-fishing, a whole host of northern Yankees employed Burma cane poles and short lengths of linen line for freshwater angling. In those days, and I am now speaking about the 20's, black bass and pickerel were more important than trout. If you ever tangle with a big pickerel you'll know why.

The tackle was crude, but it has never been topped for one particular game. The angler who planned to skitter for pickerel was ideally outfitted. For tactical reasons, the long cane and the short line is a surprisingly effective combination.

First, one had to catch bait–a few yellow perch. Angleworms sometimes worked as well, but no skittering expert ever went into action without a perch belly. This tempter was prepared by cutting a long slice from the underside of a perch, taking care to keep the fish's red anal and pelvic fins intact.

Observant sportsmen will recall that the inner wall of a perch's belly is silver. Thus the limber, carefully trimmed strip exhibits flashes of silver, yellow, red and white. It was–and it is–a highly effective bait.

In operation, an angler conned a flat-bottomed rowboat or a beamy canoe into areas frequented by pickerel and black bass: he paddled quietly, invading the shallows where lily pads spread their plastic green shields on the surface.

It was a gentle, restful sport–one that Henry Thoreau probably enjoyed on Walden Pond. It was a game divorced from the throaty roar of outboard motors. Silence was a virtue, and silence was marred only by the muted cries of lakeside birds and wild bees homing in on the pure white chalices of water lilies.

On the scene, an old time skitterer dapped and darted his perch belly or glob of nightcrawlers over the surface, through the still pools and across the jungle of water weed. Pickerel can't resist this sort of thing.

While the twisting, spattering bait dislodged bullfrogs from their lily-pad thrones, there'd be a sudden determined wake from left or right–and a boiling top-water strike. Hooked, a pickerel or bass was horsed aboard. No finesse at this point–just results.

Up to a certain point, modern anglers can emulate grandfather's tactics with a fly casting, bait casting or spinning outfit. Yet strangely, in view of the fact that most techniques are improved by modern tools, technology and the passage of years, this one is not. Cane poles are vanishing from the scene, and they remain the heart of successful skittering.

I keep telling myself that I'll buy a long, one-piece glass pole and do this job the ancient way. All else being equal, a lengthy glass rod should be better than the warped bamboo of our elders. A hank of braided nylon or monofilament will certainly take the place of twisted linen–and a perch belly is a perch belly, today or in the past.

Skittering is most effective at this season of the year, when early summer brings bass and pickerel into the shallows; when water lilies are enticing the wild, black bees; when blueberries are ripening; when springtime has succumbed to the jungle growth of deep summer.

But it's a lost art, my friends. Maybe it's well for pickerel and bass that mankind has forgotten how to skitter a perch belly across the pads. Maybe, in the interests of conservation, I ought to keep this information under my hat.

Salar!

We arrived in darkness, rattling down a precipitous, rocky trail into a gorge where the Gaspe's Grande Riviere crooned under its umbrella of sleeping trees. I had been invited to fish a privately owned salmon beat, and this in itself was a momentous thing.

Once, before Abe Lincoln's beard had grown, Atlantic salmon swarmed in all of our northeastern rivers, but dams and pollution destroyed these silvery hordes. Today, the greatest of all game fish is restricted to a few streams in Maine and to the sparkling rivers of Canada's Maritime Provinces, to Iceland and the streams of Europe's north coast.

Even in this age of strident equal rights, salmon are reserved for a select few. Anyone may fish public waters, but those areas are crowded and unmercifully pounded by the multitudes. Premier sport is still reserved for a minority of wealthy anglers, each sufficiently enamoured of the Atlantic salmon to lease or purchase entire sections of the more productive rivers. Aside from the owners, nobody fishes these beats without an invitation.

If this practice appears strangely feudal, it is worth noting that no enthusiast offers a better solution. Mass exploitation of the remaining rivers on this continent would mean the end of the grand silver migrants. Atlantic salmon simply are not plentiful enough to support a vast public sport fishery.

So, if you happen to be a poor scribbler, like me, you breathe a prayer of thanks when some Boston Brahmin delivers a gilt-edged invitation to cast a fly on storied waters. My invitation was scrawled on scratch paper by Salt Water Sportsman's publisher, Hal Lyman: "We need a fourth rod on the Grande in August. Can you make it?"

Could I!

And now—the dreaming river in the warm darkness of Canadian nighttime. No street lights here, only glittering stars overhead and the black growth pressing in. There was a clean scent of mown hay and spruce gum and clover. Then, as we approached the lodge, that acrid, old-as-time pungence of wood smoke.

It is said that a man makes one thousand casts for every salmon hooked, so we were very fortunate on that first day. Lyman was top rod with five beauties from the home pool. Dr. Perry Culver of Harvard University's Medical School came up with a pair of fifteen pounders, and I also bagged a brace. Only Dr. Charles Storey, also a Harvard don, went hungry. Later he was to score admirably.

All but one of these fish were released, unharmed—to the immense dissatisfaction of the local guides, who seem to think that a salmon brought to net should always be killed.

There was no hurry about this fishing. We ate a leisurely breakfast and motored to our specified beats at 9 A.M. Fool hens picked gravel at the road edges, white daisies and Indian paintbrush bloomed in profusion. Although it was August, there was no dulling of the summer's fresh green. Dog days are scarce in Quebec.

And then, for long, delicious hours—the river.

It flowed air-clear, deceptively deep thanks to its crystal clarity. The great salmon were there, looming like logs in their chosen lies. They had forged inland from cold northern seas, bound for the redds—the spawning grounds—far up this immaculate stream. They traveled, usually, by night, and spent the golden days resting at preordained spots.

Salmon do not feed during the annual spawning runs, but somewhere in the complex convolutions of their brains gnaws a faint recollection of days when, as parr or smolt, they gorged on the flickering insects of their natal streams.

Therefore the salmon fisherman presents a fly that simulates a memory. He presents it with care, quartering the current, mending the line, insuring that the tiny feathered artificial will swing tantalizingly ahead of a resting salmon—or, in the case of a dry fly, will drop lightly some four or five feet ahead of the slim shape and drift over the lie.

One may cast twenty times before a salmon moves, and then its interest may be indicated only by a slight shifting of position or a slight upward movement. Your heart begins to thump and it's an effort to control a piscatorial version of buck fever. The royalty of all game fish is intrigued! He settles back with a quiver of powerful fins. The fly drops lightly, sweeps down and across. Suddenly the fish takes!

It is a powerful, surging strike, quite in character with the fury of the open sea which is packed into this fish's streamlined, silvery body.

One split second later he is in the air, performing a high, graceful leap while white spray erupts and you try to remember to "bow," to drop the rod tip so that the plunging battler will not part a taut, light leader tippet. Then there is a sizzling run down through the pool, torpedoing through foaming rapids while you stumble in pursuit, rod held high, gasping with admiration at each heart-clutching jump. Finally, unbelievably, dogged resistance until this magnificent fighter is led into a waiting net.

"Let him go."

"But he's a big fish!"

"He'll be bigger next year. Let him go."

I'm for Atlantic salmon fishing, regardless of the kill. There's always a clean river and whisky-jacks to share lunch, wood smoke from the lodge at twilight and night hawks booming overhead. Invitations to share such fishing are gratefully accepted.

Where Atlantic salmon are concerned, I accept collect calls and bow three times, reverently, toward the Northeast.

The Miracle Workers

Sprawled in a lawn chair the other night, a thing I do with considerable skill, I watched a little brown bat maneuver over the dark jungle of August foliage while fireflies winked below. Man's technology performs apparent miracles, but Nature's creatures have always set the pace.

Quite suddenly I recalled that nobody has really explained the firefly's cold burst of light, an energy source that might benefit mankind were it to be duplicated.

We know how the bat vectors in on flying insects and finds its way through a maze of foliage at night. That amazing creature employs a form of natural radar, with the echoes of its thin, chittering voice bouncing back from dodging night moths and beetles.

Perched there on the shadowy lawn, with mosquitoes humming and an occasional flash of heat lightning on the horizon, I tried to think of any human technological advance that has not been predated by some curiously evolved organism of ground, air or water. There aren't many.

Men now reach for the planets, a thing no other earth creature has accomplished, yet it's worth noting that many of the systems used to further rocketry were old hat to the wild things before mankind descended from the trees.

Ben Franklin, for example, flew a kite–and why he wasn't kayoed by lightning remains a mystery. Egotistically, we like to say that the age of electricity was born with Franklin and Edison. Actually, millions of years before these titans arrived on the scene, certain eels and rays were discouraging their enemies and killing their prey with healthy jolts of electricity.

Radar, in its simplest form, goes back to the bats, and there is ample evidence that whales and other mammalian sea dwellers, such as the porpoises, employ a form of sonar. So what's really new?

Our space vehicles return to earth via parachute, a notable invention–but one long familiar to certain insects and mammals. Some spiders spin threads of buoyant silk which waft them into the air. Squirrels use their long, bushy tails as parachutes, and the flying squirrel goes one step further with loose skin stretched between fore and hind legs so that he becomes, in effect, a glider.

Pompously sophisticated, humans now take for granted the multiple banks of computers which feed navigational data to space vehicles and jet airplanes. Ornithologists are suitably impressed, but they harbor a nagging reminder that every migratory bird boasts highly efficient natural aids to navigation. No research laboratory crammed with electronic machinery yet matches the incredible accuracy of a mite-sized warbler that twitters across half a continent to nest in one infinitesimal patch of woodlot where it was hatched a year previously.

For centuries, men envied the birds. While Wilbur and Orville Wright found a way to lift human beings into the air, no mechanical creation has yet duplicated the efficiency and the operational economy of a bird's flight.

Jet propulsion startled the world of men while World War II burned to its finale, yet–if the squids of our world ocean could reason–they would be unimpressed. They've been jet-propelled for millions of years. A squid travels forward or backward with equal ease, utilizing a water jet squirted through an ideally evolved syphon system.

Man's achievements are spectacular, yet every technological development is based on natural law. We may improve upon Nature–and this is questionable–but we create nothing out of a physiological abyss. Almost always the slow, infinitely patient process of evolution has blazed a trail. Think about it!

Knights errant donned armor–long after turtles and armadillos developed thick shells and chain mail. Porcupines simulated the first phalanx of spears, so effective that any defensive strong point in a flood of attack is now dubbed a "hedgehog."

Chemical warfare, now under fire because it seems inhuman, is a johnny-come-lately. Skunks and civet cats were spraying noxious gasses while men were still battling with stones. Indeed, these aboriginal men might have learned something useful if they'd paused to observe insects scuttling into cover after a boulder had been wrenched out of the ground.

There is a very common beetle which discharges puffs of gas to discourage pursuit. You may find the *Bombardier* in any northern field, under a stone, taking his ease. He's a little guy, but centuries of evolution have made him a master of chemical warfare. While retreating, he discharges miniscule puffs of toxic smoke.

Camouflage may be the most ancient of defensive arts. There are legions of creatures subtly colored to match the hues of their native habitat, and even a few that have assumed the dress of others for specific reasons. It has been demonstrated, for example, that birds dislike the taste of a *Monarch* butterfly—so Nature has allowed the *Viceroy,* a delectable tidbit, to copy the *Monarch's* color scheme.

Even a cock ringneck pheasant, one of the most garishly plumaged of northern birds, wears camouflage. Those bright purple, burnished copper and slate gray feathers dissolve in the shadow and shine of upland cover.

Squids and octupuses, the originators of jet propulsion, have another ace up their sleeves—eight sleeves, to be exact. They employ a smoke-screen of ink to foil pursuers. The black-purple liquid confuses and dismays attackers.

Look to Nature for inspiration, and then—if you're a genius—invent something which benefits mankind. You'll be a hero, but you'd better be humble because there's very little that is new under the sun.

Indeed it may be dangerous to ridicule supposedly eccentric folk who poke around in the mold, who study wild creatures and observe curious insects found under rocks, who track the wheeling stars and dream of harnessing the sun.

Today we're proud of Robert Goddard. Never forget that, once, we thought him a harmless nut in a golf cap.

Turning Point

There is something strangely exhilarating about a cool, high-domed day in mid-August, yet any outdoorsman who follows the wheeling seasons must feel a measure of sadness in unmistakable evidence that summer is nearly over.

It hit me suddenly—as it always does—on a morning when the world had been lashed by a vicious midnight thunderstorm, then washed and dried by a cold front that swept out every vestige of drugged, tropical air.

Like that half-thrilling, half-panicky moment when one's car skids on a greasy highway, I knew that fall was in the offing. Obviously the poplars were aware of this, for each frightened, heart-shaped leaf flipped its pale underside to the cool breeze.

Miraculously, yesterday's smog and heat ghosts were gone. Lavender timothy grass rippled across Hook's lower forty and goldenrod blazed in the corners. Until this moment, lulled by the lotus-land of deep summer, I hadn't noticed an obvious change.

No matter, now that the gauntlet had been thrown, I intended to accept a challenge, to prospect the uplands and see whether our ruffed grouse were fully prepared for the guns of October. Who wants to go fishing in the fall?

And so I went hunting, but not with a gun. I spent this morning hiking the swamp edges and the uncut, forgotten fields, marveling at the fact that a storm and a cold front could so thoroughly launder an entire countryside.

In the woods, alone, I tend to talk to myself. You can make the most of this, or the worst, and I won't care. There are things I have to discuss with me, like deer tracks sharply etched in a streamside mud bank.

Arguing futilely against the demise of a season, I muttered that this whitetail would be in summer pelage, red as an old-fashioned Yankee barn. Much later, after the foliage had gone and keen winds had swept out of the north, this deer would don a "blue" shadow-gray coat.

Presently a grouse flushed, and this was the bird I had hoped to see—the very epitome of our northern countryside. Fortunately desiring, yet not entirely wanting, the onslaught of fall, it was pleasant to see four more of the brown thunderbolts whizz out almost simultaneously. This had to be an old biddy and her halfgrown brood. Summer again?

I thought so, trudging through the whispering suburban wilderness, dodging spider webs. The usual summer sounds were there—thin shreds of birdsong and a background melody of wind in the trees. Was it quite the same?

A tiny bird flitted quietly in the underbrush, then another—and another. Warblers! They were traveling southward, sampling the largess of a still-green world, but migrating to winter quarters. The warblers go very early, first of the legions, first to sense change.

Immediately I recalled that our tree swallows had forsaken the back yard, that I'd seen blackbirds flocking, that the timothy was truly lavender and the goldenrod butter-yellow. I am fond of autumn because I love the tang of gunsmoke and the fevered kaleidoscope of foliage stricken by frost, yet I hate the season for the deep-freeze it portends.

Fortunately, about noon the wind capriciously shifted southwest and the sun burned as brilliantly as ever it does in high summer. Heat ghosts reappeared over grassy fields and the foliage resumed its limp, glaucous, tropical aspect. I returned to my home and planned a fishing safari.

There'd be days, weeks, even another month of hot weather. But I knew, and the poplars knew—and so did the birds, that there is no halting the intermeshing forces of Nature.

All we can do is treasure the little that remains of a fleeting season.

Object: Salmon

We'd crossed the border at Houlton, Maine in a roaring nor'easter. New Brunswick's potato fields looked like rice paddies in a monsoon, and muddy water boiled in every stream. Conditions were hardly ideal for great fishing.

Nonetheless, Charley Whitney and I had been invited to spend the second week of September at Page Brown's camp on the Miramichi River. Charley's a retired trucker. Brown's a Pennsylvania stockbroker and sportsman. He owns a lovely stretch of water at Mercury Island, near Blissfield, New Brunswick.

In spite of muttered invocations to the Red Gods, the Miramichi was over its banks when we arrived–a brown flood littered with driftwood. Rain pattered on the roof of Page's lodge as we planned strategy for a week that began without promise.

Prospects appeared little brighter on the following morning. Although the wind had ceased and rain no longer slatted across New Brunswick's rolling hills, the clouds were low, gray and swollen. Our river was rising steadily.

Fortunately a willow branch, stuck into the mud at Mercury Island, indicated a drop in water level that night. The sun appeared for a brief moment at twilight and our hopes revived. That night Page tied a raft of flies while Charley and I made periodic trips outside to check the heavens. Before bedtime, stars were glittering overhead.

Gradually the river subsided and we began to catch salmon. Not many. The roiled water and the perverse nature of this regal fish defeated us. The odds on success seemed very long, but there are certain compensations.

There is flowing water in a green wilderness, a cold torrent which may be discolored by run-off but is never tainted with the pollution we have become accustomed to in our so-called advanced civilization.

There is a compunction to awaken at dawn, to devour platters of bacon and eggs and mugs of coffee–to feel completely healthy and alive. There is a sense of wilderness.

Few men can fail to be stirred by the mist rising from a Canadian river at dawn, blue in the shadows and gilded at the apex by a rising sun. Each morning we admired ravens flapping overhead, their wingbeats audible and strangely leathery in the sublime silence.

One green and gold morning a red fox ambled down the opposite bank to sit and watch us flailing the water. There were the whisky-jacks, very bold and eager to snatch the crust of a sandwich; ruffed grouse clucking in the spruces, and moose tracks in streamside mud.

Gradually, measured by our willow branch and by the force of current against our waders, the Miramichi relaxed its fury. The water cleared and its roar became a muted chuckle around sand bars and boulders. We caught more salmon.

All of it was magical, but that final day could have been scripted by a Hollywood hack. First off, there was no wind of consequence and the river's level had approached perfection. There was early frost, and then warm sunlight.

Upon returning to its natal stream, the Atlantic salmon is a fish that strikes at a memory. In sweet water, during its spawning run, this magnificent silver torpedo never feeds–yet occasionally reacts to a well presented artificial fly that simulates an insect devoured in the salmon's youth.

By that token *Salar* is a challenge beyond comparison. You may swim a fly past the lie of a fish many times without a strike–or he may take it avidly on the first cast. There is nothing certain about Canada's salmon *sauvage*.

Now the river was throbbing with grilse, young salmon in the four to five pound range, plus true sea-run Atlantics. For once they were hitting and we enjoyed action which is reserved for too few humans.

Margaret, Page's wife and a grand fisherwoman, splashed downstream in the wake of an acrobatic prize. Charley Whitney leaned back against a curved rod and said he never thought a man could catch salmon like bluegills. That was an exaggeration, because the law says that you can take no more than four in one calendar day.

Wading waist deep, I cast a green-butt hair fly down and across the flow, then mended line as the current swept it just above a bulge that indicated a submerged boulder. A thirteen pound hen salmon took the fly there, with the characteristic surge of power so typical of these grand fish.

One split second later the water parted to reveal a magnificent, curving missile. Battling the current, hearing line hiss off my single action reel, I scrambled ashore to follow that jet-powered beauty 100 yards down the stream into a big pool where, finally, I led it into a waiting net—and let it go. We had enough grilse for our needs, and a hen salmon might spawn generations of great gamesters.

Finally, at dusk, Page and I stood yards apart in the swift, clean Miramichi. Each of us had three salmon, one short of the limit, and it was almost time to quit.

Almost simultaneously we set the hooks in beautiful fish. Mine hit a green-butt cast right up against the opposite bank, and went flouncing down the stream, more out of the water than in. That silvery shape curved up and out, then sliced into the dark torrent time and again. Grimly, I heard the reel buzzing and felt backing whip through my fingers.

Unaccountably, he got off, and I retrieved slack line. Page was netting his prize as the shadows lengthened, and we splashed out together. It was a classic finale.

After all, if a salmon strikes at a memory, it's only fair to count a bright recollection as the grandest trophy earned by an angler.

Of Storm and Stripers

Where striped bass are concerned, Charley Whitney, an old friend of mine and now a burgher of Provincetown on Cape Cod, often seems to be in the right place at the right time. I could explain this by saying that Whitney is a good fisherman, but that would only give him a swelled head.

Some gentlefolk like to say that angling is noncompetitive, but don't you believe it. Charley and I have fished and hunted together for a lot of years, and we still try to top one another. No malice, you understand—just healthy competition.

One evening in early September, having sought striped bass through a broiling afternoon, I chose to sack out on the beach at Race Point, Provincetown. Whitney quietly launched his tin boat and went buzzing across the bay to an area natives call New Beach and newcomers recognize as Herring Cove. (In this case, incidentally, the newcomers are right, because Herring Cove was the original name—corrupted when the Town developed a bathing facility some years ago.)

Once there he proceeded to fill the skiff with nineteen prime bass, all on surface plugs. Before the following day's sun was well up, everyone on that beach knew about his catch, but the exact location of the coup was nebulous. There's a vast expanse of water surrounding the famous Race. Charley might have been down at the

Pigpens, at Second Rip, or even at Kissell's Ocean. (All are fanciful names local surfmen bestow on favored grounds. There are, in addition, The Ketchup Tree, The Portugee Shack, and High Bank.)

Few anglers clarion the location of their secret hot spots, but in view of the fact that we are old cronies, Whitney passed the magic word. If an apparently static weather front held, the same situation might obtain that night, albeit an hour later. Tides advance (or recede) by approximately 40 minutes during any 24 hour period. I said I'd be there.

It turned out to be a balmy, almost still evening. Too still. Sometimes such flat calms presage elemental fury. But the stars were bright and the wind a kiss out of the Sou'west. I pushed my surfboat into a mild wash at 10 p.m., right on the flood.

Then, aware of the fact that binoculars might be trained, I cruised northward, maintaining that course until the pinpoints of light that indicated beach buggies were long gone.

Finally, shrouded I hoped in darkness, I swung well out, turned, and twisted the throttle to full revs. The lubber line on my compass read southeast and that was just where I wanted to go. From past experience I knew that the heading would take me within a cast of New Beach.

There is a strange ecstasy in night boating, especially on an oil-smooth sea. From the shore, any darktime ocean looks entirely forbidding, but there is much light out on the offshore grounds. Certainly enough so that I could stand erect in the sternsheets, braced by an extension operating handle, and travel at full bore. There was ample visibility to dodge the occasional bit of driftwood and, later, as I angled in toward shore, to see lobster buoys floating languidly on the surface.

The tide was still slack flood. In dim starlight I could see floating strands of eelgrass, black against the silk-smooth ground swell. I made a few tentative casts and then settled back to wait. It was much too early for the promised blitz.

Presently motor sound drifted over the muted clarinets of an orchestra ashore, and then there was a silhouette to examine. Every surfboat fisherman assumes a characteristic stance. This, obviously, was Whitney who had launched well up on New Beach.

We rendezvoused—gammed in the old New England manner—and agreed that the tide would have to run for another half-hour.

"You should have been here last night!" Whitney chortled. And

then, almost as an afterthought: "We ought to get 'em when this water starts to move."

When the inshore lobster buoys were beginning to heel over in a gentle ebb tide current, I sensed change. Nothing radical. At first there was no wind other than that breath out of the Southwest, and the stars were still twinkling. Gradually, it dawned upon me that the northwestern horizon was lead colored, a somber pall that climbed higher with each passing moment.

Line squalls arrive suddenly in September, and they can be ferocious. I'd about decided to fire up and depart when the wind shifted. Now it was definitely northwest, cool, and increasing in velocity. Suddenly Race Point seemed a long way off.

Once, long ago, I'd challenged a black squall and came very close to buying it. Now, as the first maniac wind and driving rains lashed across Cape Cod Bay, I knew that this was no place for a fourteen foot tin boat.

Dimly, through the racketing gale and the lash of rain, I heard the snarl of Whitney's outboard. I cracked my own throttle wide open and ran for New Beach. We came ashore together, planing in at full bore and slamming up over the hard sand.

And it rained torrents and the surf raged and it blew like a hurricane and I had no foul-weather gear.

Charley had launched at New Beach, so his boat trailer was handy. We loaded my craft and Jeep-towed it back to Race Point. Whitney went back to find the storm ended—so he launched again, hoping to wipe my eye with a big catch.

I suppose I could spark up this account by telling how he found vast schools of stripers on the prod, and murdered them with surface plugs—but he didn't. The stripers were elsewhere.

Good thing, too, for I might have committed *harakiri* with a dull fish knife.

The Summer Sniper

The great thing about upland hunting is its lengthy season. I start "shooting" grouse in late August and never quit until January's blizzards cover our north country.

Of course most of it is in my mind, since the legal harvest doesn't get under way until October. In late August and September I carry no gun, but each flush is a new thrill. This is a time to prospect and to dream of great days afield when leaves fall and mornings are etched in hoar frost.

During high summer, those of us who dote on partridges worry about the cold rains of May and the strange cycle of life that seems to decimate this species for seven to nine years, and then to bring them back to abundance.

Glumly, in August, I noted a dearth of apples. The old, huddled trees of long-neglected farms seemed almost barren. Barberries were plentiful, but there was no great abundance of acorns. Even the huckleberries were few and far between.

Granted, midsummer divulged a better than average population of young native pheasants, a thing that would please thousands of gunners in October–but offered no solace to an ardent seeker of ruffed grouse. Those who adore partridges are almost psychotically convinced that a grouse is supreme among game birds, and that all other flyers are inferior creatures—fit only as targets for beginners. By late August I was worried.

It took a great day in September, with the first red maples flaming and a fragrant scent of wood smoke in the air, to banish self-induced qualms. Whether the famed cycle was up or down, I do not know, but it became readily apparent that Yankee partridges were still fairly plentiful in our northern uplands. I must have shot twenty in a couple of hours!

The first was a great surprise because he blasted out of an alder clump a few seconds after I'd slipped into the woods on a conditioning hike. (One must train for grouse hunting, and there's nothing quite like hip-twisting through the puckerbrush to toughen summer-softened legs.)

I got that one just as he dodged around a handy birch tree. In my mind's eye feathers were drifting, and I almost listened for the thump of a bird plunging to earth.

Moreover, still halfway convinced that our pats were in a decline, it seemed wrong to shoot. A renewable harvest is permissible, but when grouse are scarce—well, that which is taken away is no longer there.

Incredibly, a half-mile beyond this point, two battered into the air simultaneously. I hardly saw the first—just a flicker of wings through a screen of poplars—but I toppled him easily. The second towered, and that was duck soup. A clean double! A double is the nicest thing that can happen to a grouse hunter.

So I went tramping through swamp edges and over birch knolls, into the junipers and aspen slopes, around ancient apple trees that were planted by our Yankee forefathers and then reclaimed by the persistent wilderness.

Robins flitted from branch to branch. Warblers were streaming down the flyways and once I halted to train the binoculars on a curiously tame wood thrush. Of course it was also necessary to examine a porcupine's quarters and to hear the sibilant scrape of quills as that worthy retreated into his ledgy home.

Three birds had attested survival and I was content. Now, ducking under a hemlock and seeking a trail that led down to a sluggish stream in thick alders, I heard a multiple burr of wings. Three or four birds, certainly, and maybe more. I couldn't see them, so I couldn't shoot.

Briars clawed at my chino-covered legs. A deer fly buzzed in harassing circles. Hot and perspiring, I halted to dig a handkerchief out of a pocket–and that's when a whole phalanx of grouse thundered out so close that I could have touched them with the barrel of a gun. Of course I knocked down three–and I could have bagged eight or ten. I never miss under these circumstances:

They were still bunched up! Broods remain together until autumn foliage blazes, and then there is a dispersion. Before very long these young of the year would scatter like seeds from a burst pod. They'd whirl away through the woodlands; they'd smash through suburban picture windows and collide with automobiles. They'd be, as the imaginative Indians once said, indulging in "crazy flight."

This is Nature's way of scattering the broods and assuring life in new coverts. Human beings may wonder about so suicidal a movement, but we have experienced our own time of crazy flight. Think about it.

My August-September hunting is done without a gun, and yet it provides every thrill, short of that climactic moment when a charge of shot goes home and a bird falls in a smoke-trail of downy feathers.

And maybe it's better this way, because I never miss! When I swing a simulated shotgun on a rapidly departing grouse, no biddy ever goes scaling away over the hardwoods while I stand bemused in the smoke of so-called smokeless powder.

Things are different in November.

The Edge of the Unknown

At the risk of raising conservative eyebrows, I must admit to a grudging belief in sea monsters. In fact, it wouldn't surprise me to hear of an antideluvian, flippered dinosaur dredged out of the abyss. The sea is a big place, and it has a reputation for producing suprises.

Certainly there are mountainous whales and huge sharks, giant squids and snake-like oarfish measuring 30 to 50 feet in length. I have seen sawfish and bat-winged rays that looked husky enough to flatten a bass boat.

While scientists express doubt that any true sea monster exists, few are willing to declare that the creatures reported by hundreds of apparently intelligent seamen are figments of the imagination. Scoffers are reminded that, some decades back, a living coelacanth was fished out of African waters, and that additional specimens have since been captured.

The coelacanth happens to be a fish which, prior to 1938, seemed to be extinct, represented only by fossils imprisoned in million-year-old rocks. One marine biologist described the 1938 find as "an event of scientific interest comparable to the discovery of a living dinosaur."

And why not a living marine version of the dinosaur? There are men of integrity and high intelligence who accept the possibility.

Anglers generally scorn the thought, but their eyes bulge when a giant sea creature appears on the surface.

Off any northern port, if you are lucky, you will see whales that measure 70 or 80 feet from spout to flukes. Fortunately for small boat operators, the animals are not aggressive. They go their way, porpoising majestically and avoiding the buzzing outboards.

Small-boat skippers ignore leviathan, but other creatures in the sea are given a wide berth. Now, in high summer, our mariners begin to report killer whales, the orcas of the Artic, ranging down into temperate waters to harry their prey.

Killers are predators with teeth the general size and shape of bananas. They have been touted as bad medicine and, just as often, as harmless. Apparently no one knows—but an orca could engulf a small outboard, eat its occupants like hors d'oeuvres, and pick its teeth with the oars.

White sharks, which attain such respectable lengths as 20 to 30 feet, are never questioned. There is ample evidence that this species not only has dined on mankind, but has attacked small craft in order to do so. Incidence of attack, fortunately, is very low.

Nonetheless, man on the open ocean is forever aware of possible danger. In addition to the marine creatures that have been identified, one always wonders about things that have yet to exhibit themselves. And that, of course, is the sticker.

Once, anchored off Cape Cod's North Truro shore on a calm and sun-washed day, Massachusetts angler Bill Walton saw a swirl. Anglers are fond of swirls, for they usually indicate feeding game fish just below the surface. In this case, though, the swirl was 30 feet in circumference and it swept a boil of sand up from the bottom, 20 feet below. The creature involved just had to be gargantuan. Bill hauled anchor and went ashore, where he gulped a quick potion of something never recommended by Carrie Nation.

Cruising Massachusetts Bay, one afternoon in July, I observed—with some horror—the undulations of a sea serpent that could have been 60 feet long. My alleged mind was restored when the "snake's" loops resolved themselves into pilot whales, a whole porpoising pod of them playing follow the leader.

Again in the Bay I came upon a basking shark that was fully 16 feet long, and therefore two feet longer than my surf boat. This is a harmless eater of minute crustacea, yet I couldn't resist hauling out of there when the shark approached, its wide mouth gaping like the intake of a jet engine.

Baskers are benign, almost toothless hulks–but that was a big brute, and I might have flunked identification!

Often a small boat angler who fishes the sea between dusk and dawn feels like a superstitious schoolboy whistling as he lopes past a cemetery in the nighttime. The unknown is a fearsome thing.

If you're an imaginative type, out on the swelling waters when nighttime adds a measure of mysticism, when the ebony depths are flickering with the cold, blue light of microscopic dinoflaggelates, when the ground swell is breathing deeply and the inshore surf sounds like a recurrent dirge–then any sea monster is credible.

There is really no danger at all, nothing to fear.

But I keep thinking about that coelacanth, lost to the world for millions of years, and about mariners who have seen strange, snake-headed, dinosaur-shaped creatures.

One thing is certain: we still probe the edges of a last frontier.

Fall Safari

For once I did something logical. It was early October and red maples were flaming. There was a day of leisure, wherein a foot-loose bachelor might choose one of many options.

Upland hunting had begun in our north country. Striped bass were streaming down the seaboard on their annual migration to Chesapeake Bay. The calendar and the travelers indicated autumn, but it was 70 degrees in the shade and our summer foliage seemed indestructible. I went fishing close to home, seeking a species that old Daniel Webster found attractive. Obviously, Daniel was a wise man.

Some will tell you that trouting is best in springtime. Certainly there is magic in casting a fly over the freshets of apple blossom time when mayflies drift like thistledown. Spring is the beginning of it all, and our beginnings are sacred.

Inland fishermen always embrace other idols as summer's languor deepens into fall. Some enthusiasts head for the salt sea coast and some for Canada's brawling salmon rivers. By early fall a majority of sportsmen dream of bird-dogs and grouse in the birches. Me too, but circumstances alter intentions. Pause to reflect that many an impromptu adventure challenges the credits of a long planned vacation.

Early October is indecisive: if frost threatens before dawn, sun-up may find tropical temperatures wooing the dying maples. On this morning squadrons of robins owned the lawn. A wash of dew reflected diamond pinpoints of light, and the sky might have been masquerading as June. I dug a can of angleworms: they make great bait for small-stream trout.

The meadow was a sea of goldenrod, with patches of purple hardhack to offer contrast. A tiny stream trickled through bunched alders under the south slope. Drought had diminished the pools, and I wondered whether tennis shoes might have been a better choice than hip boots.

There were no human tracks in the soft mud, none of the discarded cigarette packages of May. Warblers flitted through the dusky brush and a muskrat viewed me with some astonishment before he plunged into the race that undermined an ancient stone bridge.

Happily, I threaded an angleworm on a hook, just as I had done in boyhood. Only now I employed a modern Eagle Claw hook instead of Huck Finn's japanned barb, and now I was armed with a light fiberglass rod and a spiderweb-thin monofilament line.

One does not fly-fish a tiny meadow stream, for it gurgles through a northern jungle where casting is quite impossible. Here, worming is the only profitable method, and people who scorn the use of garden hackle had best think twice. Fly fishermen make news, and smart wormers catch fish.

Moving quietly–for tramping on a brook's bank spooks nervous trout–and working with the sun in my face so that no tell-tale shadow could alarm the quarry, I became as much a stalker as a fisher of fishes.

One pool was ink-black where it reflected an overhead tangle of wild grapevines. The stream elbowed sharp right at that point, and scouring currents had gouged a deep hole under the root-armored sod.

My worm-baited hook went in quietly, well above this haven for midget squaretails, and I watched it glimmer and roll in the grip of a sluggish current. Then there was an almost imperceptible twitch, followed by a steady running-out of line.

I waited, heart thumping, disregarding the mosquito on my brow, hardly hearing a cock pheasant crowing on a distant hillside. When I brought the light rod back, sharply, there was squirming resistance.

I am not going to con you with any tale of monstrous brook trout in this ebb of the flowing year. The fish are small, measuring eight to ten inches—with an occasional trophy of twelve. But what fish!

Fall brookies are fat and deep-bodied: they are brilliantly hued in this spawning season and their flesh is pink with the good feeding of a long summer. October trout may have been pale stockees in April, but now they resemble true natives. (Any fisherman worth his salt will swear they *are* natives.)

On this day I snaked them out with no landing net, intent on harvesting enough to provide one final season's end feast. It was small-stream bait fishing at best, and I make no apology. If a white marlin must be played on 30 pound tackle, and a royal Atlantic salmon hooked on a fly—with 200 yards of backing behind the line—then there is no reason why an autumn squaretail should not be slid out of a tiny stream on a gossamer nylon line and an angleworm-baited hook.

I am very fond of Atlantic salmon, and marlin affect my heartbeat in August. All things in good time. Small-stream fishing is tranquil sport, yet it demands a full measure of skill and finesse. Finally, a brook trout in its flaming autumn coat is lovely to look at and a great delight in the pan.

I catch them on worms. Sue me! But first try it, and then you'll know the magic of a year's end safari to a tiny meadow stream.

Chinaman's Chance

The other day a cock pheasant came barreling out of a grouse cover and I nailed him before he'd reached the birch tops. He was a big bird, unbanded, so I suppose he was a native—and he'll provide better eating than a domestic capon.

But not for me. I gave that bird to a neighbor, as I do most of the pheasants bagged during an upland hunting season. Grouse and woodcock, with their immeasurably wild flavor, are more to my taste. You will have guessed, by this time, that I am prejudiced.

Most of us who specialize in ruffed grouse and woodcock scorn the pheasant as a true game bird—and maybe we lie in our teeth. The longtail is a naturalized citizen and he sometimes proves far trickier than the true native.

For my money a ruffed grouse can outfly any pheasant that ever lived. A pat is faster off the mark, more adept at dodging, and therefore more difficult to hit with a charge of birdshot.

An American woodcock is a gnome of the alders and birch runs, a tiny, moth-like bird given to strange arrivals and departures when "the moon is right" and the weather obliges. There's a sense of mystery about a timberdoodle: he's a vastly misunderstood, beloved, zigzag flyer.

All true. Also true is the undeniable fact that a grouse or a wood-cock can be brought down by a few flying pellets, while a pheasant has to be hit hard before it collapses. Score one for the ringneck: he's a tough old rooster.

On the other hand, there is no reason on this green earth for any capable gunner to miss a pheasant which flushes at close range. The fact that we all manage to miss a fair percentage of them is testimonial to the Chinaman's tactics.

A pheasant is never "just another game bird." He's a big, gaudy target and he climbs into the air with more clamor than grace. Since he's a very slow boat at lift-off, and evidently knows it, the ringneck employs nerve warfare.

He comes out of cover like gangbusters, the thunder of his battering wings laced with a high whistle as air escapes through stiff primaries. He cackles derisively, crazily, adding to the general din—and the best of gunners often find themselves mesmerized.

The tendency is to fire too quickly, aiming in the general direction of a loud glittering mark. A pheasant is all bright color—purple and gold and burnished brass. His streaming tail feathers may be twice as long as his body, hence shooters forget to compute proper lead.

In our northland ringnecks have become much sought-after game birds. They're easily reared in game farms and released to the gun. No pheasant in this country is a true native: all are the descendants of imports from Asia, purchased by the license dollars of hunters.

Some exotics fail miserably in a new habitat. Most of them simply disappear, victims of a harsh environment. Pheasants, contrarily, are now established throughout the temperate world wherever climates are roughly favorable. Tough and hardy, these great game birds quickly adapt themselves to the demands of a new territory.

Sagacious is the word for a pheasant. Unlike the native grouse or woodcock, a ringneck is an almost impossible quarry for the jump-shooter who lacks a canny bird dog. The Chinaman is a skulker, a runner and a tactician combined. Gunners harvest lots of recently stocked game-farm birds, but they experience difficulty with old roosters, wise to the ways of dogs and men.

No pheasant flies if he can hide or run. Thousands of them sit tight while shooters trudge within yards of their hiding places. Curiously, the bird's gaudy plumage becomes perfect camouflage in the shadow and shine of a weed-grown field.

Pen-reared and stocked for the gun, ringnecks quickly learn that a back yard garden is off limits to hunters. Shooters wryly observe huge roosters pattering over suburban lawns and vacant lots within the shadow of metropolis. Often the longtails seem to know where they're safe.

Unfortunately, the bird's affinity for developed land creates conflict. A minority of ignorant gunners spray the geraniums in kitchen windows, and thus insure posting by irate countrymen. It has been said that the pheasant prompts more "No Trespassing" signs than all other game birds and mammals combined. This isn't the bird's fault: it is the end result of illegal shooting by a few knuckleheads who call themselves sportsmen.

I still think that the ruffed grouse is America's greatest game bird, and that the woodcock is crown prince. I won't be swayed by colleagues, like Paul Kukonen, who are fond of noting that a pheasant is harder to flush, absorbs more birdshot before he come rattling down, is bigger, prettier (although this is a matter of opinion), and better eating than anything our north country has ever produced.

The ringneck buffs may be right, but I'll vote for grouse and woodcock. Excepting days when someone with a good bird-dog invites me to hunt pheasants.

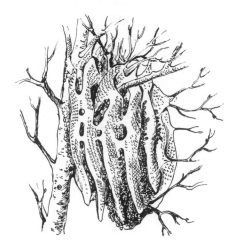

The Rebellious Bees

There is, among human beings, a strange notion that wild things are guided by instinct and never commit the sort of errors that plague fumbling mankind. It would be pleasant to believe this gentle fiction, but I have witnessed a journey into futility.

Away up in the northern birches, on a side hill which slopes to a sparkling pond, there was a house which had to fall: it was the exposed hive of a swarm of honey bees.

Hunting grouse on a golden afternoon in late October, I saw—far away in the latticework of tree trunks and bare branches—something large and opaque and bulky. For the moment my grouse were forgotten.

It might have been a raccoon, fast asleep in the afternoon sunlight, or a squirrel's nest—although bushy-tails generally construct their big, leafy nests in the crown of an oak or a hickory. In any event, I had to investigate.

There had been a succession of hard frosts and big, booming winds. Now, in this tag end of October, the foliage was about gone and the north woods were beginning to assume that stripped, barren, wiry look of late autumn.

Standing beneath the spindly birch I recognized something that is hardly rare, yet never commonplace. A swarm of domestic bees had descended here sometime in the mid-watches of spring and had built a many-layered hive in the whispering top of a swaying forest tree.

Now the temperature was just this side of freezing, and there would be more frost after the yellow sun had plunged over a poisonous green western horizon. A few bees vectored around the structure, sluggishly, and dead insects littered the ground beneath. My imagination reconstructed the saga.

They'd come here in triumph, a great crowd following a footloose queen. Back in the warmth of May or June, this legion of honey bees had split off from some farmer's hive. They'd clustered like a mahogany clot in the birch top, warmed by the beneficent sun. Gradually, as summer replaced springtime, the bees had built their waxen cells.

Now, in October, the combs were classic—subtly built, layer upon layer, molded in gentle curves like a painting by Dali. They were the pale gold of beeswax, constructed around and supported by the limber birch twigs.

All summer, from this eyrie above a warm, marginal pond the industrious insects had gleaned pollen from wildflowers and neighboring orchards. Freed from the thralldom of mankind, they had reverted to nature.

Bees, in old folklore, are wise—but these humming mites had committed a cardinal error. Had they chosen a hollow tree trunk for sanctuary there is a good possibility that the hive might have survived a frigid northern winter. Here, in the open, they were doomed.

Observing them in the chill of late afternoon, I saw a half-dozen insects succumb to the cold and come spinning earthward. Obviously this hive was dying. Could we help?

It seemed impossible, but my brother Jack and I were back on the following morning, armed with a saw, gloves and head nets. The farmer who owned this land had indicated his willingness to part with a single birch tree.

The tree came down easily enough and we lowered it without the usual crash associated with the felling of timber. A few bees investigated, but they were slow, drugged flyers, numbed by cold.

We packed the flowing combs into my station wagon and drove several miles to Jack's diggings, where we hoped that the surviving bees would move into an empty wooden hive. Passersby, on that

road, probably wondered why two men in an automobile found it
necessary to wear head nets and bulky gloves.

The effort was a failure, and perhaps this was inevitable. Cold
weather or not, the bees clung to their exposed home. They would
not embrace a new wooden hive, and they died when the temperature really plummeted in November.

But maybe they won, after all. These honey bees had been vassals
of mankind, pampered and housed in patent quarters, kept to produce honey and to pollinate orchards. No matter how you slice it,
they had been slaves. Although generations of bees, housed in
artificial wooden boxes where taut wires guided the construction of
hexagonal cells, had lost the old, miraculous skills which insure
survival—these had rebelled.

And they were all dead—the queen and the drones and the multitudinous workers. They were dead long before December's stone-
cracking cold and blizzards claimed our north country. But they
died free.

Admittedly, this is anthropomorphism, the ridiculous tendency
to ascribe human emotions to all living things under the sun. It is
pure romanticism and it is lousy science.

Actually, this was a case in which instinct (whatever that word
really means) had failed the wild things. It happens more often than
we choose to believe and it probably is an instance of those checks
and balances which continually guide natural selection.

Knowing better, I still like to think that the bees had rebelled, that
they'd swarmed free in the the burgeoning springtime and had
gloried in one magnificent summer of freedom.

If the pale golden hive was destined to die in November, who
cares? As a legendary soldier once cried—who wants to live forever!

The Eagle Gun

Crouched in a makeshift blind on the shore of Merrymeeting Bay in Maine, and waiting for a flock of Canada geese that never came, a great waterfowler of our north country caressed his 10 gauge magnum, chuckled, and said: "This is my eagle gun."

I think he was putting me on. At least I hope so.

Sportsmen may be guilty of many things, including the accidental liquidation of an occasional hen pheasant that batters out of grouse cover and is mistaken for one of the fan-tailed thunderbirds, but I know none who would deliberately kill an eagle.

This regal symbol of America is too rare for target practice. Those of us who hunt take a renewable harvest of abundant game birds, but we lower our fowling pieces when one of the harried, beleaguered species flies by.

Although relatively few citizens of the United States have ever seen a live eagle, the Audubon Society has accomplished much good in publicizing the plight of this spectacular flyer. Education, rather than law, stays eager trigger fingers.

Once the great predators were slaughtered by pioneers, and a few still fall to the guns of ignorant country bumpkins, but the rapid decline of eagle populations in our land may not be laid at the doorsteps of shooters. Nowadays it is generally concluded that insecticides and, perhaps, mercury residues, are major threats to the future of a grand and heraldic bird. The deadly poisons are far more lethal than firearms, for they kill the eaglet before it is hatched. Perhaps natural selection will insure a new race of great birds, immune to these toxic mixtures, but present odds lean toward gradual extinction.

I hope this is a pessimistic view, for even in heavily populated sections of our north country bird lovers find little colonies apparently prospering. Annually, while trolling the clean waters of New England I see a broad-winged bird far up in the blue vault of the sky. Always, for a moment, I chalk up a red-tailed hawk—and then, with a thrill of discovery, I recognize the magnificent creature that fights for survival. The bald eagle is our nation's symbolic bird: it is regally aloof, huge—somehow a living reminder of the immaculate land we continue to destroy in the forging of a super-state.

A mature bald eagle looks like an oversized hawk with somewhat disheveled feathers and a massive, curved beak: it boasts a pure white head and tail to contrast with dark wing and body plumage. Quite obviously a spirit of the true wilderness, our national talisman suffers as mankind destroys its habitat and poisons its food.

Naturalists know better, but too many well-meaning bird watchers are convinced that civilization need only restrict hunting in order to save a declining population of eagles. It isn't that easy.

First off, the "progress" which substitutes steel and cement for lush mountain valleys; the pollution which pushes a sluggish tide of death into our lakes and streams; the insidious insecticides and chemical poisons which attack an entire food change—all of these wage deadly war.

An adult bald eagle may measure nearly eight feet from wingtip to wingtip, and it requires a substantial amount of food. Much of its provender, from time immemorial, has been carrion. This, in itself, dismays incurable romantics—yet eagles have always fed on the raddled carcasses of deer killed by dogs, wolves, or simply by splitting themselves on the ice of great ponds. Beached fish are mightily esteemed, and an eagle never questions the reason why a fish has died. The pesticides kill more than noxious bugs.

Eagles regularly harry ospreys, forcing the fish hawks to drop their well-earned catch. Unfortunately, ospreys are vanishing Americans too: the same insecticides appear to be rendering them barren. Rachel Carson's *Silent Spring* is very real to naturalists who observe the grim struggle for survival.

Once, years ago, I examined an immature bald eagle which had been killed while it was in the act of snatching a chicken out of a farmyard. Such depredations are rare, but there is no doubt that the species augments its diet with poultry, rabbits and waterfowl where these are available. Any living creature inept enough to be captured and light enough to be carried aloft is fair game.

Still, the American eagle is no falcon. You'll hate me for saying so, but it is a pretty fair link between the true hawks and the buzzards.

Knowing this, I still feel a surge of elation whenever the Red Gods of the outdoors allow me to see one of these magnificent flyers wheeling regally in the lift of thermal updrafts. Our symoblic bird is more than a trademark of power: it is a reminder of the immaculate, aboriginal wilderness that each of us likes to equate with the greatness of America–the while we destroy that wilderness with the artificial lava-flow of cement and the enervating poisons of progress.

'Coon Hunt

Like Robert Frost, one cold and moon-washed night in early November, I had "miles to go before I sleep." Almost bare trees sent wiry shadows across the blacktop. Over the monotonous hum of the motor I heard a sound that awakened old memories, and I parked to listen.

Somewhere, reasonably close at hand, 'coon hounds were bugling a hot line. There were three of them, one a deep basso, one almost soprano and frenzied, and a third which yelped indecisively. The inevitable pup, I thought, not quite sure of himself.

There are worse ways to enjoy a 'coon hunt. I simply sat there with the window open, oblivious to cold air–savoring the slight scent of skunk which always seems to permeate a November woodland in the nighttime–seeing the entire affair in my imagination.

First, of course, there'd be the raccoon. He'd been foraging, leaving his almost human footprints and rank scent along the muddy banks of a swamp brook. Black-masked, luxuriously furred and highly intelligent in his own way, the 'coon had guessed the portent of that first hound voice.

Now he ran easily, well ahead of the frantic dogs, circling, backtracking, swimming black pools under the cold moon. Sometimes a wary old 'coon will turn to fight a hound in the water, and then a dog may die.

If a raccoon chooses to remain on the ground and run, a hunt like this might go on for many hours. Usually, though, the animal takes refuge in a tree. Suddenly the bugling voices of following hounds quicken to a frantic yammer. Hunters will understand—the 'coon is treed. Now it is important to arrive on the scene with utmost dispatch. Presently this happened.

Three dogs. Three golden tongues. I wondered whether they were gaunt redbones, Plotts, or perhaps Walkers. Some of the better 'coon hounds are treacherous, obeying only their masters. They are big, rangy, taciturn animals, slow moving and quiet until that vital scent of raccoon fills their snuffling nostrils.

Far back of the dogs—hunters. Perhaps they were standing close to the road, listening as I was, delighted by the wild melody of the chase. Each man would recognize the voice of his own hound.

The measured baying had become a staccato blend of yelps and strangled bugle cries. They had him treed! There'd be the lean hounds leaping, baying, almost climbing into the low branches. Above them, perched in a high crotch, his black eyes unafraid, the ring-tailed quarry—symbol of Dan'l Boone and the lost wilderness of pioneer America.

Now the hunters would be crashing in, falling over blowdowns and subversive boulders, going over their boot-tops in the chill swamp edges and hurling good natured curses into the cold November air. Barked shins and wet feet are the hallmarks of 'coon hunters and, if truth must be told, these worthies often get lost in the dark woodlands. I won't admit it to a soul, but I've been "turned around" on more than one 'coon hunt.

Enthusiasts kill a rather small percentage of the animals treed. Often the ring-tail is allowed to go his way, unmolested, after the fractious hounds have been tethered. Ruby-red eyes caught in the glow of a powerful flashlight mark the end of a great hunt. That final bullet and a furry bulk crashing down is anti-climax to many a hound man.

It is enough to hear the symphony of the dogs in full cry, to breathe the clean musk of a cold November night, to battle the clutching wilderness and, to cap it all, to give the quarry safe passage.

But now I was an armchair hunter, far from the point of decision. Perhaps these gunners sought pelts. Maybe they dreamed of raccoon roasts, a delicacy when prepared by knowing chefs. Were they beginners—anxious to kill for the sake of killing?

The air seemed colder and the moon cast an icy glow over bare hardwoods. Perhaps I'd better fire up and go home. What did it matter? The 'coon was expendable, a renewable resource, and I'd worked myself into the role of conscientious objector. It's easy with no gun in your hands.

And then the clamor ended, cut off abruptly. There was no shot, nothing but the deep sigh of November winds in high trees. They had let him go!

Suddenly I realized they had let me go, too. Should a self-confessed hunter admit compassion? At any rate, I like the idea of a live 'coon at the end of a stirring hunt.

Line of Steel

I found the steel trap where flood water had undercut a bank and some enterprising fur hunter had added a few stones to guide the path of an unwary mink. It was mid-November and the north woods were gray under a lowering sky. Thoughtfully, and without tampering, I admired the set.

It was well done. Had not some current uncovered three inches of rusty steel chain, I'd have seen nothing unusual. The lethal device was concealed by a few artfully placed dead leaves. Probably the trapper had buried a chub up under the bank. I went my way, hunting apparently non-existent grouse.

But, for the remainder of that day, like James Thurber's Walter Mitty, I dreamed of traplines and an America that has vanished. In my youth every country boy was a part-time trapper, a descendant of Kit Carson and the mountain men who explored a brand new continent.

Perhaps this latter-day fur hunter felt the same aboriginal emotion. He matched wits with the creatures of the wilderness, and he harvested rich pelts for the delight of sophisticated women. He would gorge on the romance of this business, and not on its monetary return—for trapping as a trade is disastrous.

Yet I could share his anticipation. Fur hunting—until you reach that point of reason which visualizes a trapped animal struggling for its life through the night hours—is a thrilling occupation. You must be an accomplished woodsman to succeed. You must know the habits of the quarry and be quite able to outwit its keen nose. Some animals are more sagacious than others, and the mink is no mean adversary.

Once, long ago, I followed a line of steel, and I can still recall the tremendous surge of anticipation in prospecting a marsh or stream. The neat, easily recognized tracks of a mink generated thoughts of silky fur. Muskrats were bread and butter species. All, hopefully, would be reduced to prime pelts on stretching boards.

For many of us who grudgingly accept middle age, Blake & Lamb, Victor and Oneida Jump kindle old memories. These were the steel traps we used and, so far as I know, they are still employed by fur hunters. Before you condemn a trapper, try to put yourself in his place.

He works at a killing pace, covering many miles of semi-wilderness during each day. Each set is a major gamble, a contest of human intellect against the superior nose and instinct of a wild animal. The trapper is a loner, savoring the musky woodland, exulting in his own prowess, happy only when he can outwit canny furbearers.

Whenever a trapper succeeds, I am sure that he is transported out of this mechanized, clanking Twentieth Century: he is one with Lewis and Clark, a free rover of a new world, a white brother of the Indians whose shadows still seem to populate this northern wilderness.

These things appeal to me, and therefore I spend too much time examining muskrat runs and undercut banks where mink have paid their nocturnal visits. Yet I will never trap again. Let fur farms supply pelts for the pampered women of our planet. At the very least these animals which are reared for the trade are slaughtered cleanly and without suffering.

Admittedly, my line of steel was retired because of human fraility. It is one thing to be a hunter and a booster of the clean kill: it is quite another to lie awake of nights wondering whether a muskrat or mink might be struggling to escape the iron jaws of a trap. Sportsmen, contrary to some belief, want no part of cruelty.

That night the lowering clouds spit snow. Dawn found our suburban woodlands wrapped in white. I wanted photographs of grouse (for a book I had written) yet, somewhere in the back of my mind there was this set.

I was not about to disturb it, or to frustrate the fur hunter. He had his rights, and I had mine. The odd mink was a free agent and, I suppose, he also had rights and prerogatives.

This early snow was light and soft. It clung to the trees and melted where it touched water. The stream wound through alders and birches. I was early in the woods, and few tracks profaned the new covering. There were the skittering prints of deer mice and the straightforward spoor of a red fox. Then, some fifty yards from the trap, I found the signature of a mink.

He had progressed, as is usual with this highly advanced member of the weasel tribe, close to the stream–investigating every hollow and culvert. In my mind's eye I could see him, a snake of a beast, a slim and muscular atom probing for food. Wildest of the wild, a mink is bad medicine for any lesser creature.

And then–the trap! He'd approached it without any slackening of pace. I almost expected to see a writhing, silky figure gripped in the steel jaws, but the undercut bank was silent. This mink had approached, paused–and carefully detoured.

Perhaps the trapper had left a smidgeon of his own scent, or maybe the location and the bait had been too good to be true.

I hate to admit it, for I feel a certain kinship with trappers, but my sympathies were with the mink.

Gray Day Relieved

Inevitably, a hunter sees deer just before or just after an open shooting season. This can be an unsettling experience for gung-ho types, yet there are the usual compensations.

It had rained in the morning, a cold drizzle that sifted through bare hardwoods and drenched a year's harvest of fallen leaves. By noon the clouds were lifting and I thought it wise to collect a brace of grouse for Thanksgiving.

Unfortunately, I hadn't discussed this with grouse. They proved, in this tag end of an upland gunning season, both scarce and wary.

November's woodlands are gray, at least in our north country. Occasional stands of pine and spruce may add a touch of green, but it's a green touched with shadow—muted and dirgey.

Life still teems in the woods, yet there are days when the outdoors seems swept clean. It would be easy to conclude that all game is shot out, and all protected species long gone. One must search diligently to find evidence of occupancy.

Therefore, skirting a forgotten orchard where grouse might still be feasting on moldering windfalls, I saw the dust bath of a bird— trammeled by our morning's drizzle, yet very fresh. In the exact center of this earthy bowl a fox track was imprinted.

Like me, that wraith of the woodlands was hunting. I wondered whether he also pondered an apparent emptiness, a gray and quiet

142

world of wiry brush and silvered trees—a land deserted and waiting passively for the inevitable snow.

That day not even a chickadee or a questing downy woodpecker seemed to stir. I went quietly along the edge of a big swamp, noting the fine flame of black alder's bright red berries. There, at least, was one spark of color against the pervading gray.

The carpet of fallen leaves was wet and relatively soundless. Perhaps that was why the doe never sensed my presence. Of course the wind was right—what little of it there was whispered through the brush.

She was standing in an old burn where blowdowns had fallen like jackstraws, and I looked at her for a long moment before she materialized.

That's a contradictory statement, but it's true. A deer in the woods is so magnificently camouflaged that you look right through it. Almost always the creature dimmers up like something conjured out of protoplasm. They materialize! I know no better word.

She was frozen, head turned, looking back. I froze too. The big game hunting season would not open for another week.

For an eternity, maybe two minutes, she remained a statue, then turned and picked her way through the down timber. Like all deer, she was fluid. She drifted like a gray shadow and practically poured herself over a stone wall at the end of the tract.

And that, I supposed, was all. Fortunately, weary from much tramping in search of grouse—and perhaps prone to daydream about the strangeness of the doe in an otherwise barren landscape—I remained quiet for the few minutes it took to produce a following buck.

He made no sound. Like the doe, he was gray in winter pelage, prone to appear and disappear in gray woodland shadows. Only his antlers were remarkable: not a great rack, but a good one—ash-gold in color.

Like the doe, he simply flowed over that stone wall, not bouncing over in the stereotyped manner of the regal buck. He was a sneaker all the way, a cautious, quiet romantic.

Long after he was gone I stood there, leaning against a gray birch, curiously entranced, thinking what I might have done had the big game season been open and I had a fine rifle in my hands. The woods turned gray again, and empty. The grouse were playing hard to get, so I'd eat turkey on Thanksgiving.

That's one price to pay for seeing something worthwhile. I always see better when there's no temptation to kill.

Surly Southerner

It is never very wise to incur the wrath of bird watchers, for at least 50 per cent of them are women—and everyone knows that the ladies rule our American empire. Still, there are occasions when an honest student of natural history can't help ruffling feathers.

One year, in the sports pages of a northern newspaper, I reported that a cardinal was chasing other birds from a feeder, and I stupidly referred to this handsome, crimson refugee from Dixie as a "surly southerner."

Almost immediately, a thing testifying to the power and scope of the daily press, I received a vitriolic letter from a lady in Richmond, Virginia. She not only charged me with warping the facts, but with intent to renew the War between the States!

In one sense, she was right. Research indicates that the cardinal is not an overly aggressive bird. The one I observed must have had psychological problems, for he sure as tophet chased everything from bluejays to starlings.

Things worked out well after I'd apologized, explained, and insisted that the Civil War had no bearing on my choice of the words, "surly southerner." I may be a grouchy Yankee, but I visit the Deep South each year and I can't see that, as people, we're very different.

On the other hand, some birders are really different. A few Audubon-oriented ladies are so ferociously dedicated to song birds that

146

they would sacrifice almost any other creature to see a goldfinch at a feeder.

Outdoor writers who scribble about hunting receive occasional anonymous poison-pen letters which accuse them of being "bloody-handed murderers." This hurts, but let me declare that the ladies of Audubon are not guilty. When a grande dame writes, she states her case and signs her name.

Sometimes, however, when such a champion of bird life prays for the souls of demented people who would shoot a cock pheasant during the annual open hunting season, she exhibits less charitable emotions for species that disrupt the even tenor of a feeding station.

A surprising number of these gentle people would like to have the state's wildlife technicians exterminate squirrels. There is similar, although never so vehement, thought about the proper way to treat bluejays and house sparrows. Obviously, some chemist who can produce a deadly pellet which will readily be ingested by jays, squirrels and house sparrows—but not by other birds—will be assured of fortune.

Of course squirrels are not "birds." As a harmless eccentric I claim the right to so class anything that comes to my feeder. Therefore, Woolner's meticulously kept winter list includes such "birds" as cats, dogs, weasels—and even one small boy who came armed with a stick and attempted to belt friendly chickadees out of the air.

I reasoned with the lad. He turned out to be an angling enthusiast, and his eyes got pretty big when I told him that chickadee-killers get "the curse of the kiver." They never catch anything but kivers, small ones at that, until death do them part from this mortal world.

It is reasonably well documented that lots of ardent hunters delight in the winter-feeding of birds. Some of these warriors kill squirrels during a brief open season, yet I know none who begrudge a share of sunflower seeds to bushy-tails. We may cuss 'em, but we rarely take punitive action.

Squirrels come and go. They're greedy, yet they seldom handicap small birds at a feeder. Similarly, ringnecked pheasants soak up welfare and exhibit no ill will toward the midgets. A ruffed grouse is an event: these wildest of the wild flyers usually scorn a handout.

None of the game species are shot by responsible outdoorsmen after a gunning period has ended, and a majority of nimrods would consider it less than cricket to scrag any bird brave enough to venture into the back yard, regardless of season or law. Hunters, generally, are the most zealous of conservationists during any period in which game is protected. If you want a real Puritan, look to the gunner in off-season.

It is unfortunate that sportsmen and birders cross swords. John James Audubon was, himself, a gunner—and a protector of American fauna. Modern outsdoorsmen agree with him: they want good management of natural resources, with no rape of any renewable resource. Whether hunter or bird watcher, we all desire an abundance of wildlife through wise management and conservation.

The shooter who wants to kill everything that flushes or runs is dead wrong. So is the bird watcher who urges the extermination of some species that hampers his special desires. Fortunately, exponents of either extreme constitute definite minorities.

Now I'm going out to feed my chickadees. They're getting pretty tame: in fact a couple of them insist upon landing in my fist to select the choicest of sunflower seeds.

Nobody's told them I'm one of those bloody-handed hunters who shoots game birds during a lawful season. I hope they never know.

Deerslayer

Citizens who do not hunt are puzzled by deerslayers. Why, they wonder, would anyone want to kill so beautiful a creature? Walt Disney's "Bambi" has become a sentimental symbol.

I will not argue with those who dislike hunting, not even to point out that the whitetail deer is a renewable resource. Today's controlled kill actually benefits the herd while it provides much-needed recreation for mankind—and venison for winter tables. Gunners respect the conscientious objector, while pitying him because he has never known the ageless wonder of stalking a large and wary animal in the wilderness. There is much more to a hunt than the ultimate killing of a deer.

It begins with the rough comradeship of a hunting camp, where men in red woolen underwear and flame-colored outer clothing shuck the veneer of cities to play poker in the hissing glare of gasoline lanterns. Outside, temperatures plummet in a blue-black night and a million stars glitter like frost crystals.

Dawn comes too quickly when anticipation defeats early slumber, but breakfast bacon is always sizzling long before that first magical paling of eastern skies. When it's time to hit the trail, men speak in subdued voices, as though awed by the immensity and the silence of the north woods.

Actually, there is no complete silence here: there is a continous

149

interplay of sound and color and movement. All one requires is an eye to see and an ear keen enough to sort out the multitudinous voices of the bush. Now, as always, life swarms in the big swamps and on the high ridges. There are chickadees and downy woodpeckers, their thin call notes loud in the gray forest aisles, even the whisper of their wings curiously audible.

Outdoorsmen note each sound and motion, but they do so nearly subconsciously, perhaps smiling at the antics of a red squirrel or stiffening slightly as a grouse comes hurtling out of the spruces. Might not a deer have flushed that bird?

Expert hunters must be thorough craftsmen. Beginners may not even see the quarry until the animal bounds into thick cover, flashing its huge white flag of a tail.

There are no Bambi's in the boondocks. Out where beeches flaunt yellowing foliage in otherwise bare timber, the deer is incalculably wild, magnificently camouflaged and smaller than you'd guess. An adult northern buck seldom stands higher than 36 inches at the shoulder, yet he looks as big as a draft horse in that heart-clutching moment of recognition. In November deer have lost their red-brown summer pelage; now they're woods-gray, the deep, neutral gray of a tree trunk or the blob of shadow cast by a towering hemlock.

One moves slowly in this hunting. Two steps forward, the old guides say, and then freeze for five minutes. You search for the curve of an ear, the glint of sunlight on a golden antler, the flick of a tail.

Sometimes, standing quietly where game trails meander through the woods, a deer will come to you. Then the animal seems to materialize, like a gray ghost. One moment there is nothing but a wiry maze of downed timber and trees and brush: the next, a regal buck is there!

Every hunter lives for this moment, for the sharp crack of a well-aimed rifle shot, and for the satisfaction that attends success. Still, in the end of it, I think our souls are most truly refreshed by the woods and the tiny creatures that provide a constant background of sound and motion.

One morning when the dawn had come to blanch a dark night in Maine, I was standing on a huge, cleft rock deep in the wilderness. Tiny, glittering particles of frost were drifting in the still air and the woods were quiet. Gradually I became aware of a sound,

bubbles trapped in the process of December's deep-freeze. It was a dangerous covering, thereby most enticing. We could see clean sand and weeds ten feet below our cautious boots. No law proclaimed as much, but this was an opening day.

One always moves cautiously on new ice, probing with a heavy steel chisel, feeling a delicious mixture of foreboding and adventure as the mirror cracks, crazes and sags. The ominous boom of expansion, as ice forms on a cold day, is akin to distant thunder: it's frightening until logic overcomes unreasoning terror.

Advancing in a ragged skirmish line, we spudded holes through the black glass. Two or three chisel strokes were enough, and then clean water spurted. We dropped tiny jigging spoons down into the crystal depths—and the perch were there.

Kattor whooped and hauled a struggling gamester out of its element. Warren and Bob Williams were chuckling like schoolboys, taking fish after fish. Mike Abdow and I had yet to make contact, so we concentrated on the task at hand, grimly determined to succeed.

Presently Mike was shouting in triumph, but I hardly heard him. My own spoon zigzagged into the shadowy depths, fluttered—and a slim, fish-shaped form approached. Telescopic jaws extended and the hook was sucked in. I felt pressure and lifted the jigging stick to find writhing resistance.

A yellow perch, especially a first ice perch in early December, is a thing of beauty, a symphony of green and burnished gold and ruby fins. You feast your eyes on that first conquest as it somersaults over the hard covering with gills flared, fins extended.

Perch are awfully good eating, and none are wasted. That's part of it, admittedly a very small part. The big deal is high adventure in a new season, with danger to add spice. You can get very thoroughly drowned this way, and I wish to place on record *no* recommendation for early ice fishing. If you do as I suggest, you will avoid this perilous sport.

Unfortunately, if you do as I do—you'll be there when the black ice creaks and the fish are eager.

Rabbit Hunt

Back in October the cold would have seived my bones, but acclimatization is a wonderful thing. By mid-December most of us who range the outdoors find 40 degree temperatures reminiscent of June.

A light, fluffy snow had fallen during the night–maybe three inches of the stuff, so it was a day for cowards. No need to plough through drifts or work up a sweat, yet the birds and the beasts of our suburban wilderness would leave footprint-signatured tales of high adventure.

Hoping to jump ruffed grouse, I carried a light shotgun–which was initially pointed at a bounding cottontail rabbit, but not discharged. I have long ceased to kill bunnies: they're too easy a target and sport shooting depends on a challenge.

Although our central New England woodlands boasted a dead calm, grouse seemed to be flushing wild. I found their fussy, little old lady tracks and I saw three of the feathered missiles thundering away well out of range. No frustration: they'd be there on another day, or perhaps would sire partridge phalanxes for the future.

Emerging from an alder swamp which was crisscrossed with tracks of grouse, rabbits, and the usual, ubiquitous field mice, I came to a birch and juniper-clad side hill. On the other side of this slope, following a few tentative yelps, two beagles began to sing in unison: they were hot on the trail of a rabbit.

It so happened that I had attained a little knoll which commanded the south slope of this side hill. It was an ideal stand, considering the progress of the beagles, and I wondered where their handler was stationed.

With the exception of those excited, half-strangled yelps and triumphant baying notes of the dogs, our northern woodlands seemed bereft of all sound. Tension built within me as the beagles circled, and then drove straight toward my knoll.

Nervously, I hitched the shotgun to port arms—but that was histrionics and reflex action. It would be a major breach of protocol to shoot a rabbit running in front of another man's hounds. Wherever he was, this cottontail was his "fast fish," and I wasn't about to rob him of success.

Finally the bugle notes of the two dogs, one deeper-toned than the other, swelled to crescendo. There was movement between the green junipers and I saw a cottontail soar through the concealing growth. Moments later that harried rabbit reappeared, now hopping slowly. He passed within twenty feet of my stand, and I saw his long ears twitch as he calculated the progress of the following hounds. One of those ears, unaccountably, was almost jet black.

And then the cottontail was gone and the dogs were there: they were a perfect brace, classic 13 inchers in liver, black and white. One paused to greet me. He wagged his tail, and then went bugling off into the shadow and shine of our mid-winter woodlands.

After the manner of cottontails, this bunny circled his covert, went down into the alder swamp and came back. In the end of it he must have gone to ground, for there was no shot and the rollicking, frantic voices of the beagles were extinguished as abruptly as if they had been muzzled.

Presently I went on, thinking about the strangeness of it all. A grouse flushed close enough to have qualified as a sucker shot, but I was caught off balance. Were the beagles hunting alone? That cottontail had circled the slope two or three times, yet nobody discharged a gun.

There are two species of rabbits in our woodlands. One, and I will not bore you with Latin names, prefers to remain above ground while the other holes up at any threat. There is no variety that features a single black ear, so I had seen a curious throwback of heredity. Other than this distinctive marking, the cottontail was a perfect example of its kind.

Fortunately–or I'd be wondering to this day–I met the beagler as purple shadows began to tint our birch slopes. He was a big, bluff character in a thick woolen hunting coat–so big a man that the 12 gauge shotgun under his arm looked like a toy. He had his brace of 13 inch beagles on a split leash, handsome dogs, as friendly as only this breed can be. The hunter was laconic. "Any luck?"

"Not much," I said, carefully forgetting the easy grouse I'd failed to take. "Birds are wild. Was that your rabbit up on Hook's side hill?"

"Guess so," he said noncommittally. "I had two good runs. In fact–you won't believe it–I saw a cottontail with one black ear."

I told him I not only believed it, but had seen the rabbit hop past my own shoe-pacs. Then I asked him why he hadn't killed the quarry.

For the first time this guy's big face split a wide grin. "Why didn't you?"

"Because it was your hounds, and your rabbit. Besides I don't like to kill 'em."

"That's the answer," he chuckled. "I don't like to kill 'em either. It's nice to hear the dogs work. I shoot one now and then, just to give my beagles a reason for living. Most of the time I let 'em go."

I'll buy that philosophy. Come to think of it, that's the average beagler's way of life. It is not always necessary for a hunter to kill.

Conscientious Objector

Henry Thoreau, who once described himself as a conscientious objector on a moose hunt, nonetheless declared that every young man should be a hunter. I agree, for the hunt is a magnificent conditioner in that it demands physical fitness, self-discipline and the cool marksmanship that results in a clean kill.

Moreover, in certain circumstances I applaud Thoreau as an objector. Is this maturity? Or simply the fact that a hunter, sooner or later, learns to respect the remarkable abilities and instincts of his quarry. I do not profess to know.

One evening recently, when a cold, early sunset outlined bare winter trees and the temperature was plunging toward zero, a fox barked somewhere up in the hardwoods. It was a sharp, almost metallic sound–like an axe chopping into green wood.

Why he barked, I have not the foggiest idea: perhaps he had misjudged a grouse. Maybe he was just happy in some strange, occult fox manner. His bark, at any rate, was part of the eternal wilderness, as far removed from civilization as the honking of wild geese or the mad wailing of loons on a northwoods lake.

A few outdoorsmen think that the frosty bark of a fox is his only utterance. Not so. Once I surprised a big red male on a suburban tote road in our north country–and at that time I would have squandered a week's pay to anchor a fox with a load of chilled twos.

My gun snapped up and, at that very moment, the fox screamed. There is no other word for it, although one might add a series of lurid adjectives. It was a chilling sound, a gurgling shriek of pain and rage. I never pressed the trigger.

This cry has been described by a host of woodsmen, yet it is rarely chronicled: it probably explains tales of caterwauling bobcats, panthers and evil spirits of the deep woods. The fox is a capable screamer.

Fox hunting has declined as a sport in our north woods, primarily because pelts are no longer in demand. Therein lies a testimonial to the American gunner who decries waste. Killing for the sake of killing is seldom popular, so today's fox must only outwit the beginner and the trigger-happy.

It's a wonderful game, though, full of surprises. Once, years ago when every red-blooded Yankee hunted for sport and luxurious pelts, I waited by an old stone wall as the Walkers drove a big red over the hills. Snow carpeted the ground, but the air was light and clear. The jubilant voices of those hounds came floating over a beech ridge toward me.

Presently I saw the fox: he was floating along, tail streaming like a banner. In a few short moments that cherry-red target would be close enough to kill. I held my breath and tried to remain completely motionless.

Then, unhurriedly, the fox leaped to a vantage point atop a huge boulder. Just out of gunshot range he settled on the rock to watch the hounds come on. I could see his ears perk as he lifted an astute head to study the excited Walkers as they raced along at the foot of the hill. It was as though he surveyed the efforts of his foes, and decided that their approach was bungling. In the end of it he leaped sideways and departed, still well out of range.

Last October, hunting grouse, I met a red fox at a blind barway. At twenty yards he was a gone goose, had I chosen to fire–and I think he knew it. Kill him? His pelt would have been far from prime, worth little, and I require no trophies for wall or ego.

For a long moment his strange, yellow eyes blazed into mine. Then he turned, slowly, disdainfully, and floated away with that wonderful fox gait that is the next thing to levitation.

I let him go. There is a time to kill, and another time to be a conscientious objector.

A Christmas Wish

Nobody knows what a deer thinks, if indeed these graceful animals engage in any thought process which is divorced from natural instinct. But, hag-ridden after the manner of every responsible man who hunts, I often worry about deer.

Not of the mythical Bambi's, batting false eyelashes and flaunting human emotions, but of the great American whitetail that fed and clothed a new nation more than 300 years ago, and which still provides royal sport for outsdoorsmen, fine venison and buckskin for garments which cannot be synthetized. How does it fare with deer on this Christmas day?

Certainly a measure of peace has descended upon the wilderness. Aside from an occasional poacher who knows no season, mankind now observes a long armistice with big game. But even though the guns are cased, great peril threatens wild herds. If we enjoy a white and joyous Christmas, deer—all unknowingly—face a time of torment.

Now whitetails are rolling in fat: they are sleek and vigorous, clothed in the blue winter pelage which provides almost miraculous insulation on nights when temperatures plummet and days when bitterly cold winds fracture the hardwoods. A whitetail is so well wrapped in his coat of hollow hair that he can bed down in the snow and never melt a flake under his body.

Nonetheless, snow is an implacable enemy, for a heavy fall limits the deer's range, confines the animals to beaten-down "yards," and therefore introduces the specter of starvation. Wildlife biologists have estimated that a hard winter may destroy almost two million deer in the northern United States.

Over-population triggers winter mortality, with fawns of the year dying first. Nature is a cruel taskmaster, so every animal is attuned to barometric change. Deer are consummate weather forecasters. Often as much as 48 hours before a major storm, whitetails congregate in the big cedar swamps and conifers which provide food and shelter during mid-winter months. Each buck, doe and fawn beds down as a blizzard begins, usually choosing a spot under the overhanging branches of an evergreen tree. The animals never cluster together to share warmth, although individual beds may be only yards apart.

Let it snow! Unconcerned, the wild whitetail may remain in its bed for three full days, placidly chewing its cud and gazing out through a latticework of balsam needles and cotton batting. Only when skies clear and the world is a deceptive symphony of black and white do deer arise and feed. Quite suddenly they face a destructive force which makes the guns of autumn seem merciful by comparison.

In open woodlands, regardless of season, whitetails range widely, cropping a host of shrubs which provide adequate food. A heavy snowfall disrupts all of this, for eighteen inches of the stuff dictates yarding. Now the deer are prisoners of wintertime, confined to short paths kept open by the passage of their bodies. Available food may be sufficient, if the herd is small, but overpopulation invariably leads to starvation ended by pneumonia. Fawns of the year go first, for they are not tall enough to reach available food as the browse-line climbs. There is no chivalry, no sacrifices for the youngsters—only the survival of the fittest.

Moreover, the grinding attrition of wintertime weakens all deer: that's why free-roving domestic dogs find it possible to slaughter whitetails during the seemingly endless days of February and March. By that time deer are struggling for existence. Lean of flank, bereft of autumn's fat and hampered by deep, wet snow they tire easily. The dogs, reverting back to a dim age when their ancestors hunted for food, come charging in like so many wolves. They are

steady trackers, tireless—while the whitetail is a stop and go animal. Crust supports the dogs, while the deer breaks through.

There is no doubt about it—deep snow, over an extended period of time, decimates a herd. This bitter winter covering is more lethal than the combined guns of hunters, the teeth of bobcats and the inroads of disease. If deer happen to be abundant, the snow-time kill booms in direct proportions.

If it were possible, on Christmas Day I'd promise whitetails a minimum of wintry weather. The *Old Farmer's Almanac* predicts heavy snowfall, but grouse have yet to develop "snowshoe fringes" on their feet. That's an Indian sign of a mild winter. Pray it be true, for the deer need an edge.

Wild Legacy

Out in the living wilderness this evening, on the last night of a wheeling year, deer will crop twigs and grouse will roost in the conifers. There are trout in deep, black pools, under the shielding ice of our north country. America's heritage is retained for the children of tomorrow.

In a way, this is a story in itself. We are a people who conquered a wilderness and then exploited it most ruthlessly. We made fur pay for the advance of civilization, and we decimated beaver. We slaughtered deer until it was necessary for several of the northern states to restock their covers with whitetails.

Our land use exterminated the passenger pigeon, as it did the heath hen. For a perilous balance in time, woodcock seemed destined to go the same way. Some of our wild ducks faced oblivion and were rescued at the last moment.

Now, in the final years of this Twentieth Century, wise game management has benefited all of those species capable of coping with the environment. The hunter, often depicted as a spoiler, has poured billions of dollars into conservation programs. Fishermen, similarly concerned, have added their wealth to insure that trout will rise and salmon run in the burgeoning springtime.

As a hunter and angler I am sometimes wounded by well-meaning people who rant about "bloody-handed killers." Those of us

163

who love rod and gun have spent our lives and our worldly goods to insure that no species will be shot out or fished out. Indeed, our major effort is to insure an increase, rather than a decrease, of fish and game.

Ironically, some of those who condemn the shooter and the fisher have far more scar tissue on their own consciences in the disappearances of certain species. Improper land use, the ruthless exploitation of natural resources, pollution and urban sprawl all contribute to the rapid decline of wild fish and game.

I sometimes wonder how many anti-gun legislators and well-meaning birders have invested their money in the multitudinous industries that use rivers to turn wheels and carry off poisonous affluents? How can those who wear leather shoes and eat lamb chops point a finger at the honest hunter?

Often the immutable law of natural selection is obvious. Hunting for deer in New Hampshire during the past season, I watched a pileated woodpecker in flight. The bird was positively antediluvian! It looked like the reincarnation of a pterodactl, almost reptilian with its crested head, heavy beak and slanting, ponderous flight. Prophetic?

Ivory-billed woodpeckers, a similar species, are very possibly extinct, and the pileated is far from plentiful. When the big trees go, when urban sprawl invades the north country, this spectacular bird will become a legend. It is worth noting that hunters harvest no great trees, nor do they shoot woodpeckers. Today's sportsmen are as conservation-minded as any gentle birder.

We differ only in that the huntsman believes in harvesting a renewable resource. To that end we are quite willing to ante up and to belay shooting when any species is threatened by a natural catastrophe or by human error.

When a great hurricane tumbled uncounted hollow trees that had served as nesting sites for northeastern wood ducks, back in 1938, sportsmen voluntarily closed shooting seasons and initiated a massive nesting box program that brought the handsome little waterfowl back in numbers.

Wildfowlers want lots of targets, and the only way to insure this is to provide more nesting marshes for ducks and geese. It takes money—oodles of the stuff—but shooters have never been pikers. Ducks Unlimited, for example, is an international citizen-sportsman organization which raises millions of dollars for waterfowl management.

Moreover, each duck hunter purchases a federal migratory bird hunting stamp before he fires a shell. This money is used to improve the lot of ducks and geese.

It is, or should be, common knowledge that funds derived from license fees and excise taxes pay for the propagation and release of game, for research and for management. The sportsman's dollar also pays for trout and salmon to replenish our lakes and streams. Public hunting and fishing areas, purchased with the nimrod's cash, are open to all. As hunters and fishermen, we pay the bills—and still absorb much abuse as wasters of the land's largess!

Those of us who shoot for sport have made our mistakes, but we have proved big enough to admit the fact. Years ago, gunners decimated such shorebirds as yellowlegs, plovers and sandpipers. Nowadays, these flyers are safe. They are protected by law throughout the year, and nobody shoots at them.

In the distant past we gunned too many deer, too many upland game birds and mammals. Today, intelligent management technicians decide permissible bags and lengths of seasons. Even so, citizens argue each decision made by those who administer fish and game. Invariably, the professionals find that an aroused public will permit no gamble with the well-being of a specific fish, bird or mammal.

In this shadowed final quarter of the Twentieth Century, conservation may be defined in two ways—as the sterile, often impossible maintenance of a status quo in Nature, or as intelligent management which permits a safe harvest. Obviously, hunters and fishermen vote for cautious management.

And so we can sleep well on this final night of a wheeling year. We will continue to fight for our birthright; we will attack the spoilers who use poisons and senseless land development to destroy an environment; we will preach conservation and the utilization of renewable resources within reason. And we will win.

Tomorrow the snow trails will tell us that Dan'l Boone never enjoyed so many deer, that grouse are still budding the aspens, that red foxes and raccoons and bobcats prowl the swamps and the ridges as they did when our Pilgrims moved westward. There will be game fish in our lakes and streams—because we will insist that they be there.

To one more generation, at least, we pass on the gift of a living wilderness.